INSIDER GUIDE TO THE
Niagara
Wine Region

Walter Sendzik

CANWEST BOOKS

CONTENTS

Introduction **3**
25 Things to Experience in Niagara **8**
Ontario's Wine Making Roots **17**
Taking a Wine Tour **20**
Wineries **26**
Accommodations **62**
Dining **72**
Shopping **89**
Nature Trails and Sites **94**
Tours **100**
Historical Sites **103**
Arts **108**
Glossary **114**
Map **122**

Copyright and permissions appear on pages 124 and 125

INTRODUCTION TO
Niagara Wine Country

Watching the sun set behind the rolling hills of vineyards with a couple of friends and a glass of wine is one of those moments when you wish that you could stop time. For many, a moment like this means an expensive trip to Tuscany, Bordeaux or Napa, but Canada can deliver an equally breathtaking wine country experience.

ONTARIO'S NIAGARA PENINSULA WINE REGION — WHICH IS home to more than 50 wineries — features a first-rate wine and culinary experience that can compete with the world's best. The largest of the four viticultural areas in Ontario — Lake Erie North Shore, Pelee Island and the newly anointed region of Prince Edward County — recognized by VQA Canada, the Niagara Peninsula produces more than 80 per cent of Canada's grapes for wine production.

Niagara's ability to produce such vinifera grapes as Chardonnay and Pinot Noir is the result of two natural components that frame the grape growing area – the Niagara Escarpment and Lake Ontario. Glaciers from the ice age left rich deposits of minerals and sand along the base of the escarpment providing ideal soil conditions for growing grapes. Together with the warm moderating lake effect provided by

4   INSIDER GUIDE TO THE NIAGARA WINE REGION

Lake Ontario and the protection from the height of the escarpment, grapes and tender fruit like cherries and peaches are largely protected from severe winter temperatures. Although recent cold snaps have lowered grape yields, Niagara's unique microclimate has made it possible to produce a thriving wine industry.

Within an hour's drive of Toronto and accessible from the Queen Elizabeth Way (QEW) highway, which runs through Niagara's wine country from Grimsby to Fort Erie, wine tourism in Niagara is a four season experience. Whether during bud break in the spring, the green canopies of summer, harvest of the grapes in the fall or the unique Icewine process in the winter, there's always activity at the wineries. The summer is the high season for tourism in Niagara, which is followed closely by fall as wine enthusiasts look to experience harvest up close. But winter and spring are ideal times to visit the wineries, if you are looking to avoid long tasting lines.

Capturing the essence of viticulture in the area, three popular wine festivals highlight the best of what Niagara has to offer. Every spring, the New Vintage Niagara festival spends two weeks showcasing the wineries' new releases. During the last two weeks of September, The Niagara Wine Festival, the largest wine festival in Canada celebrates the harvest. January marks the 14-day fête of Niagara's internationally recognized Icewines during the Icewine Festival.

A natural offshoot of the growth of the wine industry is the emergence of Niagara as a culinary destination. Since On the Twenty at Cave Spring Cellars in Jordan, Ontario, opened its doors back in 1993, the combination of wine paired with seasonally inspired, locally grown and made food has become a focus for many of the area's wineries and restaurants.

"Niagara offers a wine and culinary adventure that rivals the great food and wine regions of the world," says Norm Beal, president of Peninsula Ridge Estate Winery and The Restaurant at Peninsula Ridge in Beamsville, Ontario. "Visitors to Niagara have the opportunity to sample locally grown ingredients prepared by Niagara's chefs paired with some of Canada's finest wines. After travelling the world extensively, the quality of experience right here in Niagara is equal to that of Napa or even Burgundy."

A gateway to Niagara's wine country, *Insider Guide to the Niagara Wine Region* provides key information about its wineries, restaurants, attractions and accommodations. This is the ultimate guide to experiencing Niagara's wine country for day trips, weekend stays or even weeklong excursions. The Niagara Peninsula is a wine and culinary destination, one that appeals to all the senses, no matter the season.

25 THINGS
TO EXPERIENCE IN NIAGARA

The Niagara wine region has so much to offer that it may be impossible to do it all in one trip. To make sure you get the most of your visit, here is a selective list of 25 things guaranteed to enhance your Niagara wine country experience.

01 Niagara Falls
As one of the natural wonders of the world, Niagara Falls is truly majestic. The Canadian Falls is approximately 52 metres high and 675 metres wide and more than 168,000 cubic metres of water crashes over the precipice. Fireworks light up the sky every Friday night during the summer and ice formations create a frame for the thunderous Falls in winter. *Page 96*

02 Shaw Festival
Considered one of the best repertoire theatres in the world, the Shaw Festival presents the works of Bernard Shaw and his contemporaries (1856–1950). Located in the picturesque town of Niagara-on-the-Lake, the festival's three theatres offer top calibre performances from April to the end of November.
Page 113

INSIDER GUIDE TO THE NIAGARA WINE REGION

03 Niagara Parks Butterfly Conservatory

More than 2,000 butterflies inhabit a glass-enclosed rainforest setting, complete with waterfalls and ponds. In the summer, the experience also includes a butterfly garden that attracts many of the 120 species native to Ontario. *Page 98*

04 The Welland Canal

The Welland Canal is an engineering marvel; it's made up of a system of seven massive locks that lift ships between Lake Ontario and Lake Erie. Viewing platforms are located at Lock 3 in St. Catharines and Lock 7 in Thorold. *Page 107*

05 The Carousel at Lakeside Beach

Located on the beach in Old Port Dalhousie, the Carousel is one of the largest, and best maintained, Looff menagerie carousels in existence. Built in 1903, it is four rows deep with 69 carousel animals. Rides still only cost a nickel. Open during summer only. *Off Main Street, Lakeside Park, St. Catharines. www.st.catharines.com*

25 THINGS TO EXPERIENCE IN NIAGARA

06 Niagara Wine Festival

The largest wine festival in Canada takes place during the last two weeks of September. This celebration of the grape harvest in Niagara features wine tastings, tours, local cuisine and music. *1-905-688-0212. www.niagarawinefestival.com*

07 Niagara Fallsview Casino

The Fallsview Casino features a large gaming area with 3,000 slot machines and 150 gaming tables. Enjoy fine dining in 17 Noir, concerts in the Avalon Ballroom and shopping at on-site retail boutiques.
6380 Fallsview Boulevard, Niagara Falls. 1-888-FALLSVUE. www.fallsviewcasinoresort.com

08 Fort Erie Racetrack

One of Canada's most famous horse racing tracks is located in Fort Erie, just across the Peace Bridge from Buffalo, New York. The century-old track is one of the most beautiful in North America, and is home to the Prince of Wales Stakes, the second of Canada's Triple Crown races. *230 Catherine Street, Fort Erie. 1-800-295-3770. www.forterieracing.com*

10 INSIDER GUIDE TO THE NIAGARA WINE REGION

09 The Bruce Trail
Established in 1967, the Bruce Trail begins in Niagara Falls and follows the Niagara Escarpment. Running more than 850 km, it is the longest hiking trail in Canada, and it passes a number of wineries located on the Niagara Escarpment. *Page 95*

10 Niagara New Vintage Festival
The Niagara New Vintage Festival is a two-week celebration of the year's new wine releases from the local wineries. The June festival includes a gala tasting, a garden party and special events at many of the wineries. *1-905-688-0212. www.grapeandwine.com*

11 Rodman Hall Arts Centre
The historic Rodman Hall is situated within the Walker Botanical Gardens in downtown St. Catharines. Rodman Hall has a strong Canadian focus, but also includes some international artists from the 19th and 20th centuries. *109 St. Paul Crescent, St. Catharines. 1-905-684-2925. www.brocku.ca/rodmanhall*

25 THINGS TO EXPERIENCE IN NIAGARA

12 Days of Wine and Roses

During the month of February, wineries in Niagara-on-the-Lake feature special romantic offerings, including vintage wine tastings and food and wine pairings. The featured event is an elegant gala showcasing the best of food and wine from the area. *Check with individual wineries for event information.*

13 Whirlpool Aero Car

A summer attraction operated by the Niagara Parks Commission, this open-air cable car ride offers an unparalleled view of the mighty Niagara Whirlpool rapids. *Page 99*

14 Clifton Hill

Steps from the brink of the Falls, Clifton Hill is the entertainment centre of Niagara Falls. The neon-lit bright and boisterous area features more than 40 attractions teeming with family friendly activities including Ripley's Believe It Or Not Museum, Great Canadian Midway and Marvel Adventure City. *Clifton Hill between Niagara Parkway and Victoria Avenue. www.cliftonhill.com*

15 Niagara Wine Route

The Niagara Wine Route, located below the Niagara Escarpment, connects more than 50 wineries between Niagara-on-the-Lake and Grimsby. Special roadside signs mark the route making it easy to follow. *1-905-684-8070, ext. 10. www.winesofontario.org*

16 Fort George
Located just outside of Niagara-on-the-Lake, Fort George was pivotal in protecting Upper Canada against the Americans during the War of 1812. Although destroyed by fire during the war, it was restored in the 1930s. *Page 105*

17 Niagara Icewine Festival
The largest Icewine festival in the world celebrates Canada's most famous wine. For 14 days in January ice sculptures, tastings, icewine cafes, ornate ice bars and street festivals take over the region. *1-905-688-0212. www.grapeandwine.com*

18 Maid of the Mist
One of the oldest tourist operations in North America, the *Maid of the Mist* has been ferrying passengers around the basin of the thunderous Falls since 1846. Rain gear provided. Tours seasonal. *Page 96*

25 THINGS TO EXPERIENCE IN NIAGARA

19 Town of Niagara-on-the-Lake

The first capital of Ontario, Niagara-on-the-Lake, is a small historic town with a lot to offer. Often referred to as Canada's prettiest little town, it has boutique hotels, restaurants, wineries, quaint shops and the famous Shaw Festival. *East of St. Catharines and North of Niagara Falls.* www.niagaraonthelake.com

20 Niagara Falls Winter Festival of Lights

With Niagara Falls as a backdrop, one million sparkling lights, illuminated night parades, fireworks and Canada's largest New Year's Eve celebration enhance the beauty of wintertime. Runs throughout the months of November and December. *1-800-563-2557. www.wfol.com*

21 Mackenzie Heritage Printery Museum

Located in the historic home of William Lyon Mackenzie in Queenston, explore more than 500 years of printing history at Canada's largest working printing museum. *Page 106*

14 INSIDER GUIDE TO THE NIAGARA WINE REGION

22 Olde Angel Inn
Located in the heart of Niagara-on-the-Lake's Old Town, the Olde Angel Inn was established in 1789, destroyed in the War of 1812 and rebuilt in 1816. It is one of the oldest operating pubs in North America. *224 Regent Street, Niagara-on-the-Lake. 1-905-468-3411. www.angel-inn.com*

23 Jordan Village
Along the watershed of the Twenty Mile Creek, Jordan is a quaint village with a main street that features a winery, a luxury inn and Canada's first winery restaurant, along with a host of boutique shops. *Rural Road 81, Southeast of Vineland. www.jordanvillage.com*

25 THINGS TO EXPERIENCE IN NIAGARA **15**

24 Ball's Falls Conservation Area

Part of the Twenty Mile Creek, Ball's Falls was the site of grist, saw and wool mills in the early 1800s, which were all powered by the small waterfalls. The grist mill is one of the few mills in Ontario that is still in operation. A park for hiking and picnicking surrounds the falls. The area also plays host to the annual Thanksgiving Craft Show and Sale. *Rural Road 24 and 6th Avenue, South of Vineland. 1-905-788-3135. www.conservation-niagara.on.ca*

25 Winona Peach Festival

Niagara is not just grape country. Next to the vineyards are orchards that grow peaches, pears, apples, plums and many other tasty tender fruits. The annual Winona Peach Festival celebrates the peach harvest. It takes place during the last weekend in August. *Winona Park, Barton Street and Fifty Road, Winona. 1-905-643-2084. www.winonapeach.com*

Ontario's Wine Making Roots

PRIOR TO THE WAR OF 1812, A RETIRED GERMAN SOLDIER grew Labrusca grapes and made wine on a plot of land near Mississauga. Corporal Johann Schiller stands as Ontario's winemaking pioneer, though it would be more than 50 years before a commercial operation hung out its shingle.

The first commercial winery in Canada was established on Pelee Island, which is located in Lake Erie, in 1866. The remains of that building, Vin Villa, still stand today, not far from the Pelee Island Winery.

Winery development in Ontario flourished from the late-1800s to the early-1900s, when as many as 40 wineries were in operation. The industry continued to develop, even during Prohibition (1916-1927), as The Canadian Temperance Act allowed for the sale of wine – the only alcohol to be sold legally. An active bootleg trade between the border cities also meant Ontario wineries enjoyed strong, if illegal, sales to our

American cousins whose prohibition act included wine.

In 1946, Adhemar de Chaunac, who planted 40 different European grape varieties including Chardonnay and Pinot Noir in Niagara Peninsula, was the first to conduct experimentation with grapes other than the native Labrusca varieties. As late as the 1970s, growers who invested in vineyards to plant Chardonnay, Riesling, Pinot Noir and other of the so-called "noble" vinifera grape varieties were considered by some to be foolhardy. Now, we know better as many of those early vineyards are the source for the Old Vines Chardonnay and Old Vines Merlot bottlings featured in some wineries reserve portfolios.

The chief output of Ontario's wineries was a wide variety of blended wines, often labeled as ports and sherries. Many of these "wines" were popular during the '50s and '60s as they were high in sugar and alcohol. The real spark of transformation in the Ontario wine industry occurred in 1975 when Inniskillin was granted the first estate winery licence in Ontario since Prohibition. A number of estate wineries followed in its wake, including Pelee Island Winery and Colio Estates Wines, located in what is now designated as the Lake Erie North Shore viticultural area.

The inception of the Free Trade Agreement with the United States in 1988 resulted in a rapid transformation of the province's vineyards. Two-thirds of the acreage planted with Labrusca grapes were ripped out to make way for vinifera and French hybrid grape varieties. Even then suspicion of the long-term viability of vinifera grapes, such as Chardonnay, Pinot Noir, Merlot and Gewürztraminer, led to wide-scale planting of Vidal, Seyval Blanc, Maréchal Foch and Baco Noir.

A year later, the Vintners Quality Alliance (VQA) was established by 18 founding members. The alliance created a province-wide appellation system that detailed production and quality standards and regulations for winemaking. The system designated three viticultural areas: Niagara Peninsula, the area surrounding the southern tip of Lake Ontario, which accounts for 80 per cent of the country's growing volume, Lake Erie North Shore and Pelee Island.

A decade later, when the VQA Act was proclaimed into law in Ontario, there were 52 VQA producing wineries. The act cemented the quality regulations and, best of all for consumers, created an enforcement arm that oversees comprehensive audits and periodic reviews of products available at winery retail stores, LCBO outlets and at licencees. Producers are accountable that their wines live up to VQA standards. Created in Ontario and adopted by British Columbia, the VQA has established the framework for the growth and development of quality winemaking in Canada.

The growth of wineries in Ontario continues at a rapid rate. There are more than 100 winery licences currently issued in the province, including cottage fruit wineries. Meanwhile land for wine grapes in Ontario amounts to more than 6,880 hectares. Chardonnay remains the most popular single varietal followed by Riesling and Cabernet Franc. New varieties, such as Syrah, Viognier and Chenin Blanc, are coming on stream, leaving us to wonder what Ontario's vine census will look like 10 and 20 years down the line.

The future looks bright, both at home and on the international front. Niagara's industry has benefited from recently announced Franco-Canadian joint-ventures, including Le Clos Jordan, an impressive start-up created by the country's largest wine company Vincor International and the Boisset Family of Burgundy, dedicated to creating world-class Pinot Noir and Chardonnay. Canadian-born architectural visionary, Frank Gehry has been commissioned to build the winery, which will focus even greater international attention on Ontario and its winemaking capabilities. New arrivals in 2005 including Stratus Vineyards, Tawes Winery, Fielding Estates and Flat Rock Cellars continue to raise the quality bar offering wine consumers premium wines and unique experiences.

Taking a Wine Tour

EVERY BOTTLE OF WINE HAS A STORY TO TELL. FROM THE soil of the vineyards to its final blend, the journey of each bottle is as individual as the winemaker crafting it. The best way to learn about wine is to tour vineyards and wineries and what better place to start than the Niagara Peninsula, home to more than 50 wineries, almost all open to explore.

There are a variety of tours that you can take, but the length and depth depends on the size and experience of the winery. For larger wineries, such as Château des Charmes, Hillebrand and Jackson-Triggs, all of which are located in Niagara-on-the-Lake, the tour includes an in-depth look at estate vineyards through the fermentation area and into the cellars. A tour this extensive can take anywhere from a half-hour to an hour in touring time. Smaller properties offer an insider's look at the barrel room and bottling areas, which may take no more than 10 minutes.

On a guided wine tour, many of the winemaking details are the same, but it's the story behind the wineries that makes each one unique. Although you may have seen a half dozen stainless steel tanks after the first few tours, it's the guide — who could actually be the owner at smaller wineries such as Mountain Road Wine Company in Beamsville or the Strewn Winery in Niagara-on-the-Lake — who really brings out the personality of the winery.

For those looking to learn at their own pace, wineries such as Inniskillin offer self-guided wine tours with clearly marked stations that explain each step along the way.

To get a sense of the vineyards, several wineries like Pillitteri Estates in Niagara-on-the-Lake and Featherstone and Lakeview Cellars in Vineland offer tours. This is a great way to explore the soils and growing conditions that make Niagara a bountiful grape growing region. In fact, at Pillitteri — one of the oldest family-operated farms in the area — you can take a trolley ride through the estate vineyards as a guide narrates the history of this grape growing family.

Almost all tours offer an educational wine tasting, where the guide demonstrates the proper method of tasting wine. Most wineries offer public tours daily, with the larger wineries operating tours every hour or half hour, including wine tastings. While many tours are free, some wineries will charge up to $20 per person depending on the size of the winery and duration of the tour. In other cases, the tour may be free but a fee is levied or suggested for tastings — well worth the price to learn more about Niagara's oenology. Although many wineries only offer tours seasonally, winter wine tours allow participants to experience one of Canada's most highly regarded wines — Icewine.

Private tours with a personal guide are offered at select wineries, but they cost a little more and must be booked in advance. Each winery tour, whether in-depth, informal or self-guided is instrumental to appreciating the artistry required to turn grapes into fine wines.

10 *Must-Have* Essentials for a Wine Tour

1. This guide. It's your insider guide to getting the most out a wine trip to Niagara, so don't leave it at home.

2. A route map. The Wine Council of Ontario has a detailed map of wineries in Niagara and, although it only features those that are members of the organization, it's highly accurate. You can obtain a map on-line at www.wineroute.com.

3. A regional map. Getting a local map listing all of the roads in the area is a good idea in case you end up off the beaten path. Tourism Niagara has maps of the region, call 1-800-263-2988 or visit www.tourismniagara.com.

4. A schedule. With so many wineries to tour, it's imperative to map out which ones you want to visit, noting tour times and store hours making sure your schedule leaves enough time to experience each winery.

5. Palate cleansers. A bottle of water and a box of plain crackers cleanse the palate between tastings.

6. Writing materials. Bring a notebook and pen. You may be sampling many wines during the course of your visit, and jotting down notes will allow you to recall favourites.

7. Cash. Some wineries offer two to three complimentary samples of their mid-range products but may ask for a nominal fee for premium and older vintages. Ask your guide or consult the tasting menu about the winery's policy.

8. A camera. To capture the scenery of Niagara's vineyards.

9. Walking shoes. Touring vineyards and barrel cellars can be a challenge in high heels, so wear appropriate footwear.

10. Comfortable layers of clothes. Temperatures may vary from inside to outside, tasting room to cellar, so make sure you have lightweight, easy to remove and carry clothing.

Look like an Expert! 10 Questions to Get the Most Out of Your Wine Tour

ON A TOUR

What type of oak barrel is used to age the wine and how long has the wine been aged in oak?
Oak plays an important role in most red wines and a handful of whites. The two most popular types of oak barrels are made in France and America. French oak is subtler, which translates into a softer, more finessed impact on a wine. American oak is more porous, which means more of the wine has contact with the oak imparting a stronger oak essence on the wine. There are a few other countries using oak barrels including Hungary. For oenophiles looking to sample a wine made in Canadian oak barrels, visit Lailey Vineyards in Niagara-on-the-Lake, Thirty Bench Wines in Beamsville and Featherstone in Vineland. The use of oak is like a signature from the winemaker, as each winemaker has their preferences. Knowing what kind of barrels winemakers use will give you a clue about the style of the wine even before you've had a chance to sip it.

What are some techniques the winemaker uses to make its wines different?
In addition to oak aging, there are many techniques a winemaker uses to construct the wine. Chardonnay is aged on the lees. This is when the wine is aged on dead yeast cells, which imparts a creamy texture, and is often referred to as Sur Lie on the label.

Winemakers also make wines with varying levels of natural sugar, which in winemaking language is called brix. The level of brix is determined in the vineyard during harvest, and results in wines ranging from dry through to very sweet.

Another technique is blending, the process of blending specific barrels together to create a premium wine, or it can be the blending of two or more grapes together such as a Cabernet Merlot or a Gewürztraminer Riesling.

Are there many differences between this wine and those from other wineries?

This is a useful question when you want to learn about a certain grape. Take Riesling for example. Riesling is one of the few grapes that is left largely untouched from vineyard to bottle. It's an ideal grape for those searching for micro variations across a wine region. When answering questions of differences, wineries may talk about soil, climate and vineyard management to explain their approach to the wine.

What was the growing season like for a specific vintage?

Each vintage is unique. A growing season starts in the spring and ends with the fall harvest, but in Niagara some may argue that winter is part of the growing season. Understanding the growing season provides insight into the vintage. What makes a good growing season versus one that's subpar depends on the type of grape. In some years, like 2003 and 2004, white wines from Niagara shone: Both years featured cool, crisp nights during the harvest, which helped to maintain levels of acidity vital for creating crisp, flavourful white wines. Other years, such as 1998, 1999 and 2001, provided ideal conditions for red wines: Long, hot summers followed by extended warm falls, allowing red grapes for Merlot and Cabernet Sauvignon to reach their full potential.

How old are the vines that produced the grapes for this wine?

If you are in the vineyard, this is a great question as it relates to both the age of the winery and the maturity of the vine. Such older wineries as Inniskillin, Cave Spring Cellars and Henry of Pelham have vineyards with vines more than 20 years old. Older vines provide a naturally lower yield, which means the fruit is more concentrated. As well, the roots of the vines run much deeper, providing more complexity.

Do all the grapes come from one vineyard?

When browsing the shelves of wine stores, some labels refer to "estate bottled," which according to VQA standards means the wine in the bottle is made from grapes grown on the winery's property. Understanding the origins of the grapes, and if they came from one vineyard, provides better insight into what is in the bottle. For example, Coyote Run Estate Winery in Niagara-on-the-Lake offers two Pinot Noirs from separate estate vineyards with different soil types. It's a great example of the impact vineyards can have on a wine.

AT THE TASTING BAR

What varietal characteristics should I find in this wine?
Tasting at a winery isn't just an exercise in deciding if you are going to purchase the wine; it should also be an educational experience. The winery's staff is trained to answer questions and by asking about the varietal characteristics, you can get a better understanding about the wine. After a few tastings, you'll start to see the difference between a Chardonnay from Reif Estate Winery and one from Willow Heights Estate Winery.

What food should I serve with this wine?
A simple question, but it's always interesting to know which wines go best with a cut of beef or a seasoned lamb chop. Sometimes if you taste a wine varietal for the first time, like a Gamay or Baco Noir, understanding its culinary pairing partner further enhances the overall wine experience.

How long will the wine age?
According to statistics, most wines purchased are consumed within 24 hours but understanding the ageability of the wine allows you to pull the cork when the wine is showing its best.

How much does it cost?
You love a wine and you're searching for the wine boutique. Make sure you find out the price, both per bottle and case. If you are from another part of Canada or another country altogether, you may want to purchase a case of a favourite wine.

Wineries

THE NIAGARA PENINSULA VITICULTURAL AREA IS LOCATED between the Niagara Escarpment and Lake Ontario and is bordered to the west by Winona and the east by Niagara Falls. The region also includes the communities of Beamsville, Grimsby, Vineland, Jordan, St. Catharines and Niagara-on-the-Lake. While more than 50 wineries are listed, this is by no means a complete list as wineries are popping up all over the Peninsula. For ease of navigation, the wineries are listed alphabetically by region. While the information provided has been verified, it's best to call ahead.

FLATROCK CELLARS

Beamsville

Angels Gate Winery
4260 Mountainview Road, Beamsville.
1-905-563-3942. www.angelsgatewinery.com
Summer Mon. – Sat. 10 a.m. - 5:30 p.m.;
Winter Mon. – Sun. 11 a.m. - 5 p.m.
Guided Wine Tour: *Daily 11 a.m. and 3 p.m.*

Angels Gate Winery is nestled amongst lush vineyards on the rolling hills of the picturesque Beamsville Bench. The land upon which the winery was built was once owned by a Christian sisterhood, hence the name Angels Gate. With its church-inspired design and large open concept, the winery features a scenic view of vineyards with Lake Ontario as a backdrop on one side and forested woods on the other.

Dedicated to producing hand-crafted premium wines, winemaker Natalie Spytkowsky applies a less-is-more philosophy to the winery's small batch production. Located close to the Bruce Trail along the Niagara Escapement, the spotting of deer is a regular sighting leading up to harvest.

Selections include: Chardonnay, Riesling, Gewürztraminer, Cabernet Franc Icewine, Pinot Noir, Cabernets, the signature Angels III (Bordeaux blend).

Birchwood Estate Wines
4679 Cherry Avenue, Beamsville.
1-905-562-8463. www.birchwoodwines.ca
Daily 10 a.m. - 5 p.m.

Located just on the outskirts of Beamsville, Birchwood is a small, unpretentious winery. While a Birchwood forest does not surround it, the name does come from the indigenous Birchwood trees that populate the area.

Birchwood is part of a larger company, Niagara Cellars that also owns Lakeview Cellars, EastDell Estates and Thomas and Vaughan Winery. Thomas Green, one of Niagara's youngest and most talented winemakers, crafts the wines.

Selections include: Riesling, Unoaked Chardonnay, Gewürztraminer Riesling, Auxerrois, Baco Noir, Marechal Foch, Cabernet Franc, Cabernet Franc Icewine.

Crown Bench Estates
3850 Aberdeen Road, Beamsville.
1-888-537-6193. www.crownbenchestates.com
Mon. – Fri. 10 a.m. - 5 p.m., Sat. – Sun. 10 a.m. - 6 p.m.
Guided Wine Tour: *By appointment.*

Located on a crown of land near the crest of the Niagara Escarpment outside of Beamsville, Crown Bench is hidden at the end of Aberdeen Road. The farm gate winery has been converted from a house. Winemaker and owner Peter Kocsis and his wife Liva Sipos, who was named Grape Grower of the Year, an annual award bestowed by the Grape Growers of Ontario and the Niagara Wine Festival, produce small batches of estate grown wines.

For those interested in bird watching, the vineyards are an ideal spot to see hawks riding the geothermal air currents travelling up the Niagara Escarpment from Lake Ontario. Crown Bench is an ideal stop for those hiking along the Bruce Trail.

Selections include: Chardonnay, Pinot Noir, Cabernet Franc, Merlot, Late Harvest, Icewine.

Daniel Lenko Estate Winery
5246 Regional Road 81, Beamsville.
1-905-563-7756. www.daniellenko.com
Sat. - Sun. 10 a.m. - 6 p.m.

Located on the main Wine Route that runs along the Niagara Escarpment, Daniel Lenko Estate Winery is an inauspicious winery housed in a bungalow, which also happens to be the home of Daniel's parents. The Lenko vineyard in Beamsville is well known to Canadian wine buffs — the name has appeared on single-vineyard vintages since 1988. Daniel Lenko's forward-thinking father, Bill, planted vinifera grape varieties as early as 1959. The farm boasts some of the oldest Chardonnay vines in

Canada and also features old vines of Merlot, Cabernet Franc and Cabernet Sauvignon.

You'll taste some of the best wines from the region at the family kitchen table and you can finish your wine sampling with a piece of Mrs. Lenko's pie. It's a laid-back wine country experience, one that leaves the pretensions at the door.
Selections include: Chardonnay (both oaked and unoaked), Riesling, Icewine, Cabernet Franc, Pinot Noir, Cabernet Sauvignon, Cabernet blends.

De Sousa Wine Cellars
3753 Quarry Road, Beamsville.
1-905-563-7269. www.desousawines.com
May – October Daily 10:30 a.m. - 5:30 p.m.
Guided Wine Tours: *May – October 11 a.m., 1 p.m. and 3 p.m.*

Located near the top of the Niagara Escarpment, the winding, steep drive up the Escarpment to the winery is one of the most scenic landscapes in the area.

John De Sousa Jr., who inherited the winery from his father, is a third generation winemaker and he continues the tradition of crafting wines in a Portuguese style, which includes making the wines in large oak vats instead of stainless steel tanks.

The white-washed structure features a picnic area during the summer months and in keeping with De Sousa's heritage, red wines can be tasted in red clay cups. De Sousa is one of a number of wineries that pays homage to its cultural roots and demonstrates how the area's ethnic diversity has shaped Niagara's wine industry.
Selections include: Chardonnay, Riesling, Cabernet Franc, Merlot, Cabernet Merlot.

EastDell Estates
4041 Locust Lane, Beamsville.
1-905-563-9463. www.eastdell.com
Summer Daily from 11 a.m.;
Winter Tues.-Sun.
Guided Vineyard Tour: *Summer Daily.*
Winery Restaurant: The View, *Summer Daily; Winter Tues. - Sun.*

EastDell Estates commands a panoramic view of the peninsula's landscape and Lake Ontario. The winery's picturesque The View restaurant overlooks the estate's rolling vineyards. The restaurant specializes in affordable regional cuisine paired with EastDell's wines. The Bruce Trail runs past the ridge of the winery for those looking for an outdoor adventure. An in-depth vineyard tour is offered during the summer, which showcases the process of producing quality grapes and the importance of proper vineyard management.

Selections include: Chardonnay, Riesling, Pinot Noir, Cabernet Merlot, Rosé.

Fielding Estate Winery
4020 Locust Lane, Beamsville.
1-905-563-0668. www.fieldingwines.com
May – October Daily 10:30 a.m. - 6 p.m.;
November – April Tues. - Sun. 10:30 a.m. - 5:30 p.m.
Guided Wine Tour: *May – October Daily 10:30 a.m., 1:30 p.m. and 3:30 p.m.; November – April By appointment.*

Opened in June 2005, this new addition to the wineries of Beamsville is full of promise. The winemaker, Andrzej Lipinski, is one of the Canada's best young winemakers. Having apprenticed at Vineland Estates, Lipinski moved to Legends Estate winery and quickly helped establish its reputation and built his own image as a talented winemaker. With his past successes, and the focus of owner Curtis Fielding on producing small batch premium wines, Fielding Estate should become a destination for those seeking finely crafted, hard-to-get Niagara wines.

The design of the winery itself is modelled after a Muskoka cottage, giving it a distinctly Canadian-feel. Cosy and comfortable, with a tasting room overlooking a pond, Fielding Estate is an idyllic setting on the Niagara Escarpment.

Selections include: Chardonnay, Riesling, Pinot Gris, Merlot, Cabernet Franc, Pinot Noir, Syrah.

Legends Estate Winery
4888 Ontario Street North, Beamsville.
1-905-563-6500. www.legendsestates.com
May – October Daily 10 a.m. - 7 p.m.;
November - April Mon. – Fri. 10 a.m. - 6 p.m.,
Weekends 11 a.m. - 5 p.m.
Guided Wine Tour: *By appointment.*

Established in 1946, this family-owned farm and winery is now in the hands of the third generation, Paul Lizak. Located just inland from Lake Ontario, the winery has more than 80 hectares planted with both grapes and a variety of other fruits. A relatively new winery, Legends is recognized as one of the best small craft producers of VQA wines.

Selections include: Chardonnay, Riesling, Gewürztraminer, Pinot Noir, Cabernet Franc, Cabernet Sauvignon, Cabernet blends, Late Harvest, Icewines.

Magnotta
4701 Ontario Street, Beamsville.
1-905-563-5313. www.magnotta.com
Mon. – Wed. 9 a.m. - 6 p.m., Thurs. – Fri. 9 a.m. - 7 p.m.,
Sat. 9 a.m. - 6 p.m., Sun. 11 a.m. - 5 p.m.
Guided Wine Tour: *Mon. – Fri. 2 p.m.*

Magnotta's retail store offers a glimpse into one of Niagara's largest wine producers. With its head office located just outside of Toronto in Vaughan, most of the wine's production takes place outside of Niagara. The boutique features a presentation area, art gallery, as well as a look at the distillation of a selection of fine spirits that is also part of Magnotta's production. An art collection features works by many local Niagara artists.

Selections include: Chardonnay, Riesling, Sauvignon Blanc, Pinot Gris, Vidal, Pinot Noir, Cabernet Franc, Cabernet Sauvignon, Baco Noir, Late Harvest, Icewines, including a Sparkling Vidal Icewine.

Maplegrove Vinoteca Estate Winery
4063 North Service Road, Beamsville.
1-905-856-3200. www.toronto.com/vinoteca
By appointment.

Another satellite operation, Maplegrove Vinoteca's main operations are located in Toronto. A retail outlet is located at the company's vineyard site in Niagara. The name of the winery is a combination of the Italian "Vino" (wine) and "Teca" (a chest for special treasures), which is a celebration of the owner's, Giovanni and Rosanna Follegot, Italian heritage. The Niagara location is a small bungalow on the north side of the QEW between the highway and Lake Ontario.
Selections include: Chardonnay, Pinot Gris, Riesling, Cabernet Merlot.

Mountain Road Wine Company
4016 Mountain Street, Beamsville.
1-905-563-0745. www.mountainroadwine.com
Daily 10 a.m. - 6 p.m.
Guided Wine Tour: *By appointment.*

Steve Kocsis, the third of the Kocsis cousins in Niagara to open a winery in Beamsville, arrived at the family farm in 1958 and planted his vinifera vines in 1983. Prior to opening his own winery, his vineyards supplied grapes for some of Niagara's wineries including the wines of Thirty Bench Winery and Tempkin-Paskus since 1991.

As an amateur winemaker and grape farmer who is passionate about the land and devoted to his vineyards, Kocsis crafts wines for this small boutique winery that express the essence of the land.

Selections include: Chardonnay, Riesling, Vidal, Gamay, Cabernet, Baco, Marechal Foch.

Peninsula Ridge Estates
5600 King Street West, Beamsville.
1-905-563-0900. www.peninsularidge.com
May – October Daily 10 a.m. - 6 p.m.;
November – April Mon. – Fri. 11 a.m. - 5:30 p.m.,
Sat. – Sun. 10 a.m. - 5:30 p.m.
Guided Wine Tour: *11:30 a.m. and 3 p.m.*
Winery Restaurant: The Restaurant at Peninsula Ridge,
Wed. – Sun. 11:30 a.m. - 10 p.m.

    Owned and operated by Norman Beal, Peninsula Ridge is forging its reputation with small batches of Chardonnay, Sauvignon Blanc, Bordeaux-style reds and Syrah. With French winemaker Jean-Pierre Colas, formerly of Domaine Laroche winery of Burgundy, Peninsula Ridge embraces the best of Old World winemaking techniques and the finest in modern technology.

    Nestled on the Niagara Escarpment near Grimsby, Peninsula Ridge covers more than 30 hectares and features three unique facilities: a retail shop and tasting bar located in a restored 1885 post-and-beam barn with an impressive underground barrel cellar, a beautifully restored Victorian home that houses the winery's restaurant, and Coach House for private and corporate meetings, dining functions and intimate weddings.

Selections include: Chardonnay, Sauvignon Blanc, Merlot, Cabernet Franc, Cabernet Merlot, premium Bordeaux blends.

Thirty Bench Wines
4281 Mountainview Road, Beamsville.
1-905-563-1698. www.thirtybench.com
April – November Daily 10 a.m. - 6 p.m.;
Dec. – March Daily 11 a.m. - 5 p.m.
Guided Wine Tour: *By appointment.*

    Thirty Bench is located near the Thirty Mile Creek on the Beamsville Bench. Founded by winemakers/partners, Tom Muckle, Yorgos Papageorgiou and Franz Zeritsch, the winery has developed a loyal following for its ultra-premium wines. Recently purchased by Andres Wine Company, which also owns Peller Estates and Hillebrand Estate Winery, Thirty Bench offers an intimate tasting experience. With its rustic, cedar-sided design, the winery's philosophy is more about what's in the bottle rather than the size of its tasting room. Surrounded by rolling vineyards, it's a wonderful place to stop, sample and enjoy the view that stretches all the way to Lake Ontario.

Selections include: Chardonnay, Riesling, Pinot Gris, Merlot, Cabernet Franc, Cabernet Sauvignon, Bordeaux blends.

Thomas & Vaughan Winery
4245 King Street, Beamsville.
1-905-563-7737. www.thomasandvaughan.com
Daily 11 a.m. - 6 p.m.
Guided Wine Tour: *By appointment.*
Wine Tour: Self-Guided *May – October*

Recently purchased by the owners of EastDell Estates, Thomas & Vaughan was founded by Barbara Vaughan and Thomas Kocsis. The husband and wife team established the cottage-style winery as a vineyard-to-bottle production focusing on quality accessibly priced wines. Located on the main Wine Route through Beamsville.

Selections include: Chardonnay, Vidal, Cabernet Sauvignon, Baco Noir, Cabernet Merlot.

Grimsby & Winona

Kittling Ridge Estate Wines & Spirits
297 South Service Road, Grimsby.
1-905-945-9225. www.kittlingridge.com
Mon. – Sat. 10 a.m. - 6 p.m., Sun. and Holidays 11 a.m. - 5 p.m.
Guided Wine Tour: *June – September Tues. - Fri. 2 p.m., Weekends and Holidays 11 a.m. and 2 p.m.*

Winemaker and owner, John Hall has been crafting wines and spirits since the mid-1980s. The winery first started out as a distillery producing fruit brandies, vodkas and whiskeys but in 1993 the distillery was awarded a licence to produce wine and the name was changed from Rieder Distillery to Kittling Ridge Estate Wines & Spirits.

The wine shop offers a wide selection of wines, including Canada's first and only Icewine Brandy.

Kittling Ridge also produces a line of flavour-infused vodka and whiskey, but it's the wines that should get you to detour into Grimsby.

Selections include: Chardonnay, Merlot, Cabernet Sauvignon, Baco Noir, Icewine Brandy, a host of red and white blends.

Puddicombe Estate Farms and Winery
1468 #8 Highway, Winona.
1-905-643-1015. www.puddicombefarms.com
May – December Daily 9 a.m. - 5 p.m.
January – April Mon. – Fri. 9 a.m. - 5 p.m., Sat. – Sun. 10 a.m. - 4 p.m.;
Guided Wine Tour: *June – October 11 a.m. and 1 p.m.;*
November – May By appointment.

This 200-year-old fruit farm owned by the Puddicombe family became a winery in the 1940s. Today the winery is run by Lindsay Puddicombe, one of Niagara's youngest winemakers. Located just outside of Stoney Creek, the farm gate winery also features a general store offering freshly baked pies, as well as jams and maple syrup, for sale. There are also plenty of activities for children including Lil' Pud, Niagara's first agricultural train and a tractor-pulled wagon.

Selections include: Riesling, Viognier, Chardonnay, Sauvignon Blanc, Gamay, Cabernet Sauvignon, Pinot Noir, Merlot.

Jordan

Cave Spring Cellars
3836 Main Street, Jordan.
1-905-562-3581. www.cavespring.ca
June - October Mon. – Wed. 10 a.m. – 6 p.m.;
Thurs. – Sat. 10 a.m. – 7:30 p.m., Sun. 11 a. m – 6 p.m.;
November – May Mon. – Thurs., 10 a.m. – 5 p.m.;
Fri. - Sat., 10 a.m. – 6 p.m., Sun. 11 a.m. – 5 p.m.
Winery Tours: *June – October Daily 12 p.m. and 3 p.m.;
November – May Sat. – Sun 3 p.m.; private tours by appointment.*
Winery Restaurant: On the Twenty, *Daily lunch and dinner.*

Located in the historic Jordan Winery building on Main Street, Cave Spring is a large part of Jordan's unique small town experience. The one-street village features the winery, its wine boutique, On the Twenty winery restaurant and an inn and spa. It also has antiques, garden and home décor shops, a café, and a museum. The village of Jordan makes for a great outing.

Founded in 1986 by the Pennachetti Family and winemaker Angelo Pavan, Cave Spring Cellars controls one of the oldest blocks of vinifera vines in Niagara, dating back to the mid-1970s. Pavan has crafted some of the finest Rieslings and Chardonnays produced in the region, including his top-end estate-bottled CSV wines. He is equally adept with red wines, especially Gamay and Cabernet Franc-based Bordeaux blends.

Cave Spring is also one of Canada's most internationally established wineries. With distribution in fine wine shops and restaurants in the U.S., U.K. and Europe, the winery is quickly forging a name in these markets, especially for its stellar Rieslings. The winery's philosophy is that under-appreciated varietals such

as Riesling and Gamay will put Niagara's name on the wine map of the world.
Selections include: Chardonnay, Riesling, Pinot Gris, Pinot Noir, Gamay Noir, Cabernet Merlot, Late Harvest Riesling, Riesling Icewine.

Creekside Estate Winery
2170 4th Avenue, Jordan Station.
1-877-262-9463. www.creeksidewine.com.
May – September 10 a.m. – 6 p.m.;
October – April 10 a.m. – 5 p.m.
Winery Tours: *May – September 2 p.m. Daily.*

Perched along the Sixteen-Mile Creek between Jordan and St. Catharines, Creekside Estate Winery is owned by Laura McCain Jensen and Peter Jensen. Opened in 1998, the winery has emerged as one of the area's top producers of Sauvignon Blanc, Chardonnay and Pinot Noir. It's grown from a 3,000-case production to 30,000-case production and now boasts Canada's largest underground barrel cellar. Lead by the talented winemaking duo of Australian Craig McDonald and Canadian Rob Power, the wines are classic examples of the quality coming from Niagara's Bench vineyards.

In 2005, the winery entered into a partnership to produce a line of wines for Canadian golfer Mike Weir, who is planning to open a winery of his own in the area in the near future.

In the summer, a patio overlooking the creek offers gourmet lunches and special events.

Selections include: Chardonnay, Sauvignon Blanc, Pinot Gris, Riesling, Pinot Noir, Cabernet Sauvignon, Cabernet blends, Icewine.

Flat Rock Cellars
2727 Seventh Avenue, Jordan.
1-905-562-8994. www.flatrockcellars.com
May – October Daily 10 a.m. – 6 p.m.;
November – April Sat. – Sun. 10 a.m. – 6 p.m.
Winery tours: *By appointment.*

Located just off the main route outside of Jordan, Flat Rock is tucked up on the rolling hills of the Niagara Escarpment and is only a few minutes from the village of Jordan.

Opened in May 2005, Flat Rock Cellars is one of Niagara's most architecturally beautiful wineries. Designed to showcase the land from which the grapes are harvested, its pentagon-shaped glass-walled tasting room offers a panoramic view of the Niagara Escarpment and Lake Ontario. On a clear day, it's one the best vistas in the area.

The winery is dedicated to Riesling, Chardonnay and Pinot Noir. This state-of-the-art gravity-flow winery allows the wine to flow naturally during the entire process of winemaking from crush to bottling.

One caveat that may surprise visitors, Flat Rock caps all its wines with a screw cap to prevent cork from tainting the product and it's the first winery in Canada to place a screw cap on icewine.

Selections include: Chardonnay, Riesling, Pinot Noir, Icewine.

Harbour Estates Winery
4362 Jordan Road, Jordan Station.
1-877-439-9463. www.hewwine.com.
Summer 10 a.m. – 6 p.m.; Winter Noon – 5 p.m.
Winery Tour: Self-guided tour through the vineyard along a path that leads to a scenic lookout over Jordan Harbour. Organized tours including eco-tours, winemaking tours and vineyard tours; reservations required.

Situated off the QEW, Harbour Estates is located in Jordan Station, a town named after its original train station. Owned by Fraser Mowat, Harbour Estates Winery sits on a unique site more than nine metres above Jordan Harbour (where the Twenty Mile Creek enters Lake Ontario). The vineyard is planted with Cabernet Franc, Cabernet Sauvignon and Merlot grape vines, which are supplemented by white grape varieties acquired from local growers. Mowat's son, Ken, another of Niagara's emerging young winemakers, leads the winemaking team.

Focusing attention on its scenic setting, the winery has developed a series of nature trails. During the summer, visitors can picnic at the winery, taking in a scenic view of the bay at the back of the vineyards. As well, each year, Harbour Estates hosts two special events: a rock 'n' roll wine event during the Niagara Wine Festival and the annual Great Grape Stomp – a past winner is Ben Mulroney, host of *Canadian Idol*.

Selections include: Chardonnay, Riesling, Sauvignon Blanc, Vidal, Cabernet blends, Baco Noir, Icewine.

Thirteenth Street Winery
3983 13th Street, Jordan Station.
1-905-562-9463. www.13thstreetwines.com
Sat. – Sun. 10:30 a.m. – 5 p.m. or by appointment.
Located near the village of Jordan. This petite winery takes its name from the street on which it is located.

Thirteenth Street Wine Company was founded in 1998 by the Douglas, Funk, Jacobson and Willms families, all of whom have been active in the wine industry either as growers or amateur winemakers for several decades.

Since it's opening, the winery has garnered much attention for its small lots – it produces only 1,500 cases – of estate grown wines. It's not a large operation and there are no fancy tours, it's simply a place to stop and taste product from a vineyard with a passion for creating great wines.
Selections include: Chardonnay, Riesling, Gamay Noir, Pinot Noir, Sparkling.

Niagara-on-the-Lake

Caroline Cellars
1028 Line 2, Niagara-on-the-Lake.
1-905-468-8814. www.lakeitfarms.com
Mon. - Sat. 10 a.m. - 6 p.m., Sun. 11 a.m. - 6 p.m.

Caroline Cellars is a rustic cottage winery located in a custom-built post-and-beam barn. The small production operation has an intimate tasting room and loft for special occasions. Fairly new on the scene, the winery was recently opened by the Lakeit family, who has been growing grapes in the area for four generations.
Selections include: Chardonnay, Vidal, Riesling, Cabernet Franc, Merlot, a number of French hybrids, Riesling Icewine.

Château des Charmes Wines
1025 York Road, Niagara-on-the-Lake.
1-905-262-4219. www.chateaudescharmes.com
Daily 10 a.m. - 6 p.m.
Guided Wine Tours: *Daily 11 a.m. and 3 p.m.*

Located furthest from the centre of Niagara-on-the-Lake, Château des Charmes has the distinction as being the only Niagara-on-the-Lake winery that rests on the lower bench of the Niagara Escarpment. An elder of the area's wineries, it was founded in 1978 by Paul Bosc, a fifth generation winemaker and grower from France, who, along with his sons, Pierre-Jean and Paul-Andre, produce the wine. The winery, surrounded by estate vineyards, is a replica of a French château — complete with a long driveway leading up to the copper-roofed building.

It specializes in Bordeaux and Pinot Noir reds and Chardonnay, Aligoté and Burgundian whites. Many of the winery's highly acclaimed wines are single-vineyard from the St. David's Bench and Paul Bosc Estate vineyards. An excellent touring facility offers a first-hand look at how wines go from the vine to the bottle.

Selections include: Chardonnay, Riesling, Aligoté, Viognier, Sauvignon Blanc, Pinot Noir, Cabernet Merlot, Cabernet Sauvignon, Sparkling Wine, Select Late Harvest Riesling, Riesling Icewine.

Coyote's Run Estate Winery
485 5th Concession, St. Davids.
1-905-682-8310. www.coyotesrunwinery.com
May – October Daily 10 a.m. - 6 p.m.;
November – April Daily 10 a.m. - 5 p.m.

Situated close to Château des Charmes, Coyote's Run is just off the QEW on the outskirts of Niagara-on-the-Lake.

Opened in May 2004, the winery is owned and operated by Jeff and Patti Aubry and Steven Murdza. The winery is surrounded by 23 hectares of vines, which have been tended to by the

Murdza family for more than 50 years. The winery's name was derived from the numerous coyotes that run through the vineyards during the harvest.

With a focus on small batch, hand-crafted wines, this estate winery doesn't have all the bells and whistles of the larger names, but the wines have received numerous accolades, especially the Pinot Noir, Chardonnay and Cabernet Franc.

Selections include: Chardonnay, Riesling, Pinot Noir, Cabernet Merlot, Vidal Icewine, Riesling Icewine.

Frog Pond Winery
1385 Larkin Road, Rural Road 6, Niagara-on-the-Lake.
1-905-468-1079. www.frogpondfarm.ca
Tues. – Sat. 1 - 5 p.m.

Frog Pond holds the distinction of being Ontario's first and only fully certified organic winery. The small, rustic farm is located close to Marynissen and Inniskillin wineries.

Former Stonechurch Vineyards winemaker, Jens Gemmrich and his wife Heike Kock operate Frog Pond following the principles of organic farming, which means they do not use insecticides, herbicides, synthetic fungicides or chemical fertilizers. The wines are also processed and certified by Organic Crop Producers and Processors. Because the winery is only a few years old, there's not much of a back vintage and its releases are limited.

It's best to call ahead to make sure wines are available and it's open to visitors.

Selections include: Riesling, Cabernet Merlot.

Hillebrand Estates
Highway 55, Niagara Stone Road, Niagara-on-the-Lake.
1-905-468-7123. www.hillebrand.com
Daily 10 a.m. - 6 p.m.
Guided Wine Tours: *Daily on the half hour.*
Winery Restaurant: Hillebrand Estates Vineyard Café, *Daily lunch and dinner.*

Hillebrand is one of the most established wineries in Niagara. Owned by Andres Wines, who also owns Peller Estates, Hillebrand is a large winery operation with a collection of buildings that house the winemaking facilities, wine shop, barrel cellar and winery restaurant.

With meticulous attention to detail, the winery is an ideal destination for both wine newbies and enthusiasts. In-depth winery tours are conducted by well-trained staff and the wine shop is spacious, accommodating large groups.

The Hillebrand Estates Winery Restaurant overlooks the vineyards and barrel cellar. More casual than the formal setting of Peller Estates Restaurant, Hillebrand also offers impeccable food and service. The winery also hosts two popular annual events, a jazz festival in July and blues festival in August.

Selections include: Chardonnay, Riesling, Sauvignon Blanc, Cabernet Franc, Cabernet Sauvignon, Merlot, Late Harvest, Icewine.

Inniskillin Wines

Niagara Parkway at Line 3, Rural Road 1, Niagara-on-the-Lake. 1-905-468-3554. www.inniskillin.com
May – October Daily 10 a.m. - 6 p.m.;
November – April Daily 10 a.m. - 5 p.m.
Guided Wine Tour: *May – October Daily 10:30 a.m. and 2:30 p.m.; November – April Weekends only 10:30 a.m. and 2:30 p.m.*
Self-Guided Wine Tour: Well-marked and informative self-guided tour takes you through the winemaking process.

Located between Niagara-on-the-Lake and the village of Queenston, the venerable Inniskillin Wines is the birthplace of the modern wine industry in Ontario. It received the first winery licence issued by Ontario since 1929 — the beginning of Prohibition Era — on July 31, 1975. Since then co-founders Donald Ziraldo and Karl Kaiser have blazed a trail producing European-style wines in Ontario.

Inniskillin achieved international fame when it won the prestigious Civart Trophy at VinExpo in France in 1991 for its 1989 Vidal Icewine. The award brought world-wide attention to Niagara for its Icewine and, as a result, Inniskillin has become the most well-known Canadian winery on the international stage.

The name Inniskillin was inspired by local historical events. Colonel Cooper led a British regiment during the War of 1812 called the Inniskilling Fusiliers. After the war, the Colonel was granted land along the Niagara River, which he named Inniskillin Farm.

The wine shop is located in the estate's Brae Burn Barn, which was built in the 1920s. The historic barn has a design that was influenced by the work of famous architect Frank Lloyd Wright. Surrounding the winery is the Brae Burn vineyards. Brae Burn means "hill stream" in Gaelic. The production facility is adjacent to the barn and its design also complements the historic nature of the winery.

Around the back of the winery, where the old water tower is located, Canadian artist Charlie Pachter's installation replicating the Niagara Escarpment is a must-see for those interested in Canadian art.

The winery also offers one of the best self-guided tours in the region. With well-placed and informative stations throughout the winery, visitors are encouraged to walk through the facility to see how wine is made. The winery also boasts a private tasting room and barrel cellar featuring Inniskillin Icewine vintages dating back to the early '80s, not to mention a collection of custom-made Inniskillin Icewine bottles that the winery commissions annually from Canadian glass artists.

Of special note, the vineyards adjacent to the Niagara Parkway are recently planted Riesling vines that will go into a limited edition Riesling Icewine with a portion of the proceeds to benefit Canadian Olympic athletes.

Selections include: Chardonnay, Riesling, Pinot Grigio, Pinot Noir, Cabernet Franc, Merlot, Cabernet Sauvignon, Late Harvest Vidal, Vidal Icewine, Riesling Icewine.

Jackson-Triggs Niagara Estate Winery

2145 Niagara Stone Road, Highway 55, Niagara-on-the-Lake.
1-866-589-4637. www.jacksontriggswinery.com
Daily 10:30 a.m. - 5:30 p.m.
Guided Wine Tour: *May – October Daily 10:30 a.m. - 5:30 p.m. every half hour; November – April Sun. – Fri. 11 a.m. - 4 p.m. every hour, Sat. 10:30 a.m. - 5:30 p.m. every half hour.*
Tasting Gallery: Daily offering cheese, fruit and bread plates.

Owned by Vincor, the largest wine company in Canada and the fourth largest in North America, Jackson-Triggs is the largest winery in Niagara. The winery is a fine illustration of how both quality and investment has turned Niagara's wine country into a world-class destination.

The modern design of Jackson-Triggs set it apart from the area's other wineries when it was opened in 2001. The state-of-the-art facility was designed by Kuwabara Payne McKenna Blumberg Architects of Toronto as an environmentally sensitive building and is made of only three materials: wood, concrete and steel. Landscape features include a native-plant garden and a water feature modelled after the Niagara River.

Guided tours by knowledgeable staff are offered daily starting in the Great Hall and moving past the vineyards, the crush pad, the production facility and into the barrel cellar — the curvaceous arches framing the oak barrels is a captivating site.

Jackson-Triggs hosts a series of special event dinners called Savour the Sights. Guests are treated to a movable feast: a dinner where each course is served in a different part of the winery. During the warm summer months, the winery also hosts concerts in an open-air amphitheatre located in the back of the vineyard.

Selections include: Chardonnay, Riesling, Sauvignon Blanc, Gewürztraminer, Pinot Noir, Cabernet Franc, Merlot, Cabernet Sauvignon, Cabernet Merlot, Sparkling Wine, Vidal Icewine, Riesling Icewine, Cabernet Franc Icewine.

Joseph's Estate Wines
1811 Niagara Stone Road, Rural Road 3, Niagara-on-the-Lake.
1-866-468-1259. www.josephsestatewines.com
May – October Daily 10 a.m. - 7 p.m.;
November – April 10 a.m. - 6 p.m.
Guided Wine Tour: *May – October Daily 11 a.m., 1 p.m. and 3 p.m.*

Dr. Joseph Pohorly, a pioneer in the Niagara wine industry, opened the winery in 1992. Pohorly also founded the Newark Winery in Virgil in 1979, which later became Hillebrand Estates, and it was at Hillebrand in 1983 where he made one of Canada's first Icewines.

Joseph's Estates is a small boutique winery with a casual, friendly atmosphere. With associate winemaker Katherine Reid, Pohorly offers a wide selection of wines from traditional red and whites, sherry, port and fruit wines.

The winery is also next to Picard's Nut Store, a great place to stop for a bag of Niagara grown nuts.

Selections include: Chardonnay, Riesling, Vidal, Cabernet Franc, Late Harvest, Icewine.

Konzelmann Estate Winery
1096 Lakeshore Road, Niagara-on-the-Lake.
1-905-935-2866. www.konzelmannwines.com
May – October Mon. – Sat. 10 a.m. - 6 p.m., Sun. 12 p.m. - 6 p.m.;
November – April Mon. – Sat. 10 a.m. - 5 p.m., Sun. 12 p.m. - 5 p.m.
Guided Wine Tour: *May – September Daily at 2 p.m.;*
Self-Guided Wine Tour: *Available year-round.*

Touted as Niagara's only lakefront winery, Konzelmann Estate Winery is located between Niagara-on-the-Lake and St. Catharines. Herbert Konzelmann, seeking to replicate the fine wines of Germany in Niagara, established the winery in 1984. Considered a pioneer in the industry, Konzelmann, who comes from five generations of winemakers, introduced German winemaking and vineyard techniques to the area. The tasting room has touches of its German influences in its décor, as do the wines themselves.

The wine shop is situated at the front of the lakeside property with the estate vineyards reaching back towards Lake Ontario. The

vineyard has a picnic area at the back of the estate, from which you can see Toronto across the lake on a clear day. A notable event is the annual Konzelmann barbeque held every July, which features German foods paired with Konzelmann wines.
Selections include: Chardonnay, Riesling, Pinot Noir, Merlot, Cabernet Sauvignon, Cabernet Merlot, Late Harvest, Icewine.

Lailey Vineyard
15940 Niagara Parkway, Niagara-on-the-Lake.
1-905-468-0503. www.laileyvineyard.com
May – October Daily 10 a.m. - 6 p.m.;
November – April Daily 11 a.m. - 5 p.m.
Guided Wine Tour: *By appointment.*

Lailey Vineyard is a small estate winery situated near the landmark McFarlane Home and Park just on the outskirts of the Old Town. The intimate winery features a small tasting station on the first floor, and a larger tasting/tutoring room on the second floor overlooking the estate vineyards.

The Lailey family has been an integral part of the modern wine industry in Niagara. William Lailey planted some of Niagara's first French hybrid varieties back in the early 1950s. In 1970, David Lailey and his wife Donna purchased the farm and started its transformation into a top-rated vineyard. Donna Lailey was recognized for her contributions to vineyard advancements in Niagara when she was crowned Grape Queen, an annual award of the Grape Growers of Niagara.

The winery specializes in Pinot Noir and Lailey was one of the first wineries to experiment with Canadian oak. Tastings of Canadian, American and French oaked Chardonnay and Pinot Noir can be sampled at the winery, subject to availability. Also notable is that as of 2003, Lailey is herbicide free, which means it has eliminated the use of chemicals to control the weeds in the vineyard.

Selections include: Chardonnay, Riesling, Pinot Noir, Cabernet Merlot, Cabernet Franc, Cabernet Sauvignon.

Maleta Estate Winery
450 Queenston Road, Niagara-on-the-Lake.
1-905-685-8486. www.maletawinery.com
Daily 10 a.m. - 5 p.m.

Maleta winery is a small cottage-style winery. With its operations in a small hut and wine shop located in a converted house, there's not much to see — but there are a few gems definitely worth tasting. On a historical note, the winery is adjacent to one of Niagara's earliest wineries, the Sunnieholme Winery, which was established in 1918, but is now defunct and used as a storage garage.

Selections include: Chardonnay, Riesling, Meritage, Gamay, Vidal Icewine.

Marynissen Vineyards
Rural Road 6, Concession 1, Niagara-on-the-Lake.
1-905-468-7270. www.marynissen.com
Daily 10 a.m. - 6 p.m.

Marynissen has been a small estate winery since 1990. Considered an early pioneer of vinifera grapes in Niagara, John Marynissen began planting European grapes in Niagara in the 1970s. In fact, he was the first to plant Cabernet Sauvignon in 1978, and those vines are now among the oldest in the area. The winery is now operated by John's daughter Sandra.

Throughout the '90s Marynissen developed a reputation as a premium red wine producer. With small batches that were often made from specific lots of vineyards surrounding the winery, the Marynissen label became highly sought after.

Selections include: Chardonnay, Cabernet Sauvignon, Cabernet Franc, Merlot.

Niagara College Teaching Winery
135 Taylor Road, Niagara-on-the-Lake.
1-905-641-2252. www.nctwinery.com
Daily 10 a.m. - 6 p.m.

The Niagara College Teaching Winery is the only winery of its kind in Canada. Dedicated to teaching the art and science of winemaking, the winery is part of a unique campus that also specializes in cuisine, viticulture, horticulture and ecology. The wines are crafted by the College's emerging winemakers under the guidance of a professor and all proceeds from the sale of the wines go to providing more equipment for the students. The wine shop is connected to the horticultural centre, which has plants for sale. Wine tours and wine tastings are available.

On-site greenhouse, gardens and Wetland Ridge Trail linking to the Bruce Trail, all help illustrate the beauty of the Niagara Peninsula. The newly opened Niagara Culinary Centre features a restaurant with a wine list including those made at the College.
Selections include: Chardonnay, Riesling, Pinot Noir.

Peller Estates
290 John Street East, Niagara-on-the-Lake.
1-888-673-5537. www.peller.com
Summer Daily 10 a.m. - 9 p.m.;
Winter Daily 10 a.m. - 6 p.m.
Guided Wine Tour: *Daily, on the hour.*
Winery Restaurant: Peller Estates Restaurant, *daily lunch & dinner.*
The closest winery to the Old Town, Peller Estates is within walking distance of the Shaw Festival's main theatre. The jewel in crown of the Andres Wine Company's wineries, Peller Estates captures the rich tradition of the Peller family in Canada. Founder of Andres Wines, Andrew Peller was a significant player in the development of Canada's wine industry. Now the family winery is under the guidance of grandson and current CEO, John Peller.

The large, beautifully constructed winery features a French château-influenced design with an impressive foyer and a grand fireplace to welcome visitors. The spacious wine boutique offers wine enthusiasts an opportunity to shop for wine and accessories. The barrel room has a private dining area that overlooks the winery's barrel collection. As well, there's a private tasting area on the second floor featuring vintage wines from the library collection. Although there are no winemaking facilities on the site, it's a fitting monument to one of Canada's great winemaking pioneers.

For those looking for a culinary experience, the Restaurant at Peller Estates overlooks the winery's vineyards and the surrounding Niagara Escarpment. The formal dining room features seasonal fare paired with estate wines. During the summer an outdoor patio offers a more casual setting.

Selections include: Chardonnay, Riesling, Sauvignon Blanc, Cabernet Franc, Merlot, Cabernet Sauvignon, Late Harvest, Icewine, Sparkling Wine.

Pillitteri Estate Winery
**1696 Highway 55, Rural Road 2, Niagara-on-the-Lake.
1-905-468-3147. www.pillitteri.com**
May 15 – October 15 Daily 10 a.m. - 8 p.m.;
October 16 – May 14 Daily 10 a.m. - 6 p.m.
Guided Wine Tour: *Daily 12 p.m. and 2 p.m.,* summer tours include a trolley tour of the vineyards.

Owned and operated by the Pillitteri family since 1993, the winery celebrated its 10th anniversary with the opening of an immense underground barrel cellar. The facility also includes a retail boutique, country market with outdoor patios and spacious meeting rooms for private group tours and special functions. Special events include seasonal weekend barbecues and trolley tours, tutored wine tastings and food and wine pairings.

The patriarch of the family, Gary Pillitteri, came to Canada from Sicily in 1948. As an amateur winemaker, Pillitteri won a number of awards including a gold medal for Icewine. In 1993, he opened the winery and began producing quality, estate-grown wines.

More recently, Pillitteri winemaker Sue-Ann Staff has emerged as one of Canada's brightest young winemakers. In 2002, she was the first female winemaker to win the Ontario Wine Award Winemaker of the Year and she was short-listed for Female Winemaker of the Year at the London Wine and Spirits Competition in 2005.

Proud of its history and achievements, Pillitteri displays its many awards from around the world at the entrance to the winery. Here, a floor-to-ceiling display case houses the coveted Civart Trophy from the Challenge International du Vin, in Bordeaux, France, and a rare Double Gold Medal from the American Wine Society, both for the winery's roster of Icewines. Currently, Pillitteri is Canada's largest producer of Icewine.

Selections include: Chardonnay, Pinot Grigio, Riesling Gewürztraminer, Cabernet Franc, Merlot, Cabernet Sauvignon, Late Harvest, Sparkling Icewine, Vidal Icewine, Riesling Icewine, Cabernet Franc Icewine.

Reif Estate Winery
15608 Niagara Parkway, Niagara-on-the-Lake.
1-905-468-7738. www.reifwinery.com
May – October Daily 10 a.m. - 6 p.m.;
November – April Daily 10 a.m. - 5 p.m.
Guided Wine Tour: *May – September Daily at 1:30 p.m.*

With the best spot on the Niagara Parkway, Reif Estate Winery is located between Niagara-on-the-Lake and the village of Queenston. The winery sits beside the historic Grand Victorian Inn near the Niagara River.

Opened in 1983 by Klaus Reif, the winery's architecture reflects Reif's German heritage. Hailing from a long family history of winemakers, Reif came to Canada in 1977 and planted vines along the river. Specializing in estate-grown wines, Reif and co-winemaker, Roberto DiDomenico are dedicated to producing quality wines. In 2002, Reif won the prestigious Grand Gold medal at

the VinItaly and a gold medal at the Wine and Spirits Competition held in London, U.K. for its 2000 Vidal Icewine.
Selections include: Chardonnay, Riesling, Gewürztraminer, Pinot Noir, Cabernet Merlot, Late Harvest, Icewine.

Riverview Cellars
15376 Niagara Parkway, Niagara-on-the-Lake.
1-905-262-0636. www.riveviewcellars.com
June – September 10 a.m. - 7 p.m.;
October – November 10 a.m. - 6 p.m.;
December – March 10 a.m. - 5 p.m.; April – May 10 a.m. - 6 p.m.
Guided Wine Tour: *By appointment.*

Located a stone's throw from the Niagara River, Riverview has one of the most scenic locations in Niagara-on-the-Lake. Closer to the village of Queenston than the Old Town, Riverview is a quaint winery that offers a select number of wines.
Selections include: Chardonnay, Riesling, Cabernet Sauvignon, Cabernet Franc, Late Harvest, Icewine.

Stonechurch Vineyards
1242 Irvine Road, Niagara-on-the-Lake.
1-866-935-3500. www.stonechurch.com
November – April 10 a.m. - 5 p.m., Sun. 11 a.m. – 5 p.m.;
May – October 10 a.m. - 6 p.m., Sun. 11 a.m. - 5 p.m.

Stonechurch takes its name from a local historic church built in the 1850s by the Empire Loyalists. Located just off of Lakeshore Road, it's the closest winery to the Welland Canal. The winery is nestled among the vineyards and it features a spacious retail store, private tasting and function rooms, outdoor patio, gazebo and picnic area.

Stonechurch offers self-guided vineyard tours, weekend barbecues in the summer and many special events such as the evening Star Gaze Craze and Cruisin' Car Sundays.

Selections include: Chardonnay, Sauvignon Blanc, Cabernet Sauvignon, Cabernet Merlot, Icewine.

Stratus Wines
2059 Niagara Stone Road, Niagara-on-the-Lake.
1-905-468-1806. www.stratuswines.com
May – October Daily 11 a.m. - 5 p.m.;
November – April Wed. – Sun. 12 p.m. - 5 p.m.

The newest winery in Niagara-on-the-Lake, Stratus opened its doors in June 2005. Situated beside Jackson-Triggs, just before the Old Town, Stratus is a state-on-the-art winemaking facility dedicated to producing premium and ultra-premium wines. With 21 hectares of vineyards and the winemaking talents of J. L. Groux, who previously crafted some of Niagara's finest reds with Hillebrand Estates, Stratus is positioned to be one of Niagara's best top-end wineries.

The tasting room alone is worth the visit. Designed by renowned Canadian interior designer, Diego Burdi, the modern and spacious area features floor-to-ceiling windows, a sleek tasting bar and open-rack shelves. Adjacent to the tasting room is a terrace overlooking the vineyard.

In terms of tasting, Stratus has developed a unique tasting program, which consists of three comparative 'flights' of wines served in premium crystal stemware. Flights are $10. As well, Stratus features weekly, thematic seminars based on the art of pairing wines, foods and cheeses.

Selections include: Stratus Red and Stratus White, Chardonnay, Merlot, Cabernet Franc, Cabernet Sauvignon, Riesling Icewine.

Strewn Wines
1339 Lakeshore Road, Rural Road 3, Niagara-on-the-Lake.
1-905-468-1229. www.strewnwinery.com
Daily 10 a.m. - 6 p.m. Guided Wine Tour: *Daily 1 p.m.*

Strewn is a unique destination for wine and food lovers. The location is a beautifully restored canning factory that has been transformed into a winery, cooking school and restaurant.

Owner and winemaker Joe Will and his wife Jane Langdon have created a winery and culinary experience combining premium estate wines with an interactive cooking school, the only winery cooking school in Canada.

A spacious wine shop and separate tasting area can accommodate large groups. The cooking school offers a wide array of classes for everyone from novice gourmands to kitchen commandos.
Selections include: Chardonnay, Riesling, Sauvignon Blanc, Cabernet Franc, Cabernet Sauvignon, Cabernet Merlot, Late Harvest, Icewine.

St. Catharines

Harvest Estate Winery
1179 4th Avenue, St. Catharines.
1-905-682-0080. www.harvestwines.com
Daily 10 a.m. - 6 p.m.

Located on the outskirts of west St. Catharines, Harvest Estate Winery shares space with Harvest Barn, which specializes in selling local produce and features a bakery, deli and salad bar.

The winery, owned by Hernder Estates, offers a wide range of affordably priced wines, including fruit and dessert wines. Harvest Estate is only a wine shop, so there are no tours or winemaking facilities on site. An outdoor picnic area makes for an ideal space to stop for a quick lunch on the wine route.
Selections include: Chardonnay, Vidal, Cabernet Franc, Baco Noir, Late Harvests.

Henry of Pelham Family Estate Winery
1469 Pelham Road, St. Catharines.
1-905-684-8423. www.henryofpelham.com
May – October Daily 10 a.m. - 6 p.m.;
November – April Daily 10 a.m. - 5 p.m.
Guided Wine Tour: *Daily 1:30 p.m. or by appointment.*

Henry Pelham is located on the curvaceous Pelham Road, which runs along the Niagara Escarpment and the Bruce Trail outside of downtown St. Catharines. The family-run winery is one of Niagara's most recognized, due to the hard work of the three brothers who run the business – Paul, Matt and Daniel Speck – along with talented winemaker, Ron Geisbrecht. Back in 1984, while still in high school, the brothers helped their late-father plant the vineyard on the winery site, which has been in the family for six generations.

The Henry of Pelham Family Estate Winery was named after a distant relative of the Speck family, Henry Smith – known as Henry of Pelham in the area – who built an inn on the site in 1842.

The winery's tasting rooms and retail store are housed in the old inn. Rustic and unpretentious, the site has been enhanced with the addition of the Coach House Cafe, which offers a large selection artisanal Canadian cheeses. In July, the vineyards become the backdrop for Henry of Pelham's annual Shakespeare in the Vineyard event.

Selections include: Chardonnay, Riesling, Pinot Noir, Cabernet Merlot, Baco Noir, Late Harvest Riesling, Riesling Icewine.

Hernder Estate Winery
1607 8th Avenue, St. Catharines.
1-905-684-3300. www.hernder.com
Mon. – Fri. 9 a.m. - 5 p.m., Sat. – Sun. 10 a.m. - 5 p.m.
Guided Wine Tour: *Daily 1:30 p.m. and 3:30 p.m.*

Tucked away, just off Seventh Street South between Pelham Road and Regional Road 81, is Hernder Estate Winery. Founded in 1991 by Fred Hernder, whose family has been growing grapes since 1939, the winery is housed in a circa-1867 barn. Travel over Niagara's only covered bridge and down the winding driveway to the charming stone and post-and-beam structure.

The winery also has a barn housing the two large banquet rooms, which is a popular wedding and events spot. During the summer months, the winery's large patio features weekend barbecues and live music. Hernder produces a wide selection of traditional and fruit wines.

Selections include: Chardonnay, Riesling, Gewürztraminer, Cabernet Franc, Merlot, Cabernet Sauvignon, Baco Noir.

Vineland

Featherstone Estate Winery
3678 Victoria Avenue, Vineland.
1-905-562-1949. www.featherstonewinery.ca
April – December Fri. - Mon. 10 a.m. - 6 p.m.

Perched on the brow of the Niagara Escarpment, Featherstone Estate Winery is owned and operated by husband and wife team David Johnson and Louise Engel. In their pre-grape lives, the duo owned a culinary market in Guelph called the The Guelph Poultry Gourmet Market. In his free time, Johnson honed his skills as an amateur winemaker. In 1999, the pair moved from Guelph to their current home.

Located just up the hill from the village of Vineland, the winery is dedicated to producing small batch, premium wines from grapes that have been cultivated on their 23 acre insecticide-free vineyard. In 2003, the Grape Growers of Ontario named the vineyard Vineyard of the Year, and David was awarded the prestigious Grape King title.

In keeping with Featherstone's pesticide-free practices, Engel has trained a red-tailed hawk called Amadeus to help control the bird and rodent population who help themselves to grapes during the harvest.

Selections include: Chardonnay, Riesling, Gewürztraminer, Vidal Blanc, Cabernet Franc, Merlot, Gamay Noir, Vidal Late Harvest, Vidal Icewine.

Kacaba Vineyards
3550 King Street, Vineland.
1-905-562-5625. www.kacaba.com
May – October Daily 10 a.m. – 6 p.m.;
November – April Daily 11 a.m. – 5 p.m.
Guided Wine Tours: *By appointment.*

Poor urban planning has reduced the amount of agricultural land available in Niagara by close to 50 per cent over the past 30 years. In 1997, Michael Kacaba found a vineyard location that was slated to be a sub-division, and after a protracted legal battle, he succeeded in saving the land.

Located on the main wine route, just outside of the village of Vineland, the entrance to the winery is framed by Niagara ledge rock from the Niagara Escarpment. Travelling up the driveway, an iron bridge takes guests over a picturesque ravine.

The small estate winery offers an intimate tasting room. In the summer, you can wander the vineyards just beyond the wine store, and catch a glimpse of Lake Ontario and beyond.

Selections include: Chardonnay, Riesling, Pinot Gris, Gamay Noir, Pinot Noir, Merlot, Cabernet Sauvignon, Meritage.

Lakeview Cellars Winery
4037 Cherry Avenue, Vineland.
1-905-562-5685. www.lakeviewcellars.on.ca
May – October Daily 10 a.m. - 5:30 p.m.;
November – April Mon. - Sat. 11a.m. - 5 p.m., Sun. Noon - 5 p.m.
Guided Wine Tour: *By appointment.* Includes a vineyard tour, weather permitting. Patio open through the summer.

Lakeview Cellars opened in 1991, when amateur winemaker Eddy Gurinskas decided to make his wines available to the masses after winning a number of amateur winemaking awards. The transition pleased the palates of many wine consumers. Over the years, Gurinskas' winning ways continued with many awards recognizing his ability to craft wonderfully bold and brawny Bordeaux-style red blends and complex Chardonnays.

Situated on 13 acres along the Beamsville Bench area of the Niagara Escarpment, the winery has a commanding view of the rolling hills of the Escarpment down to Lake Ontario. A few years back, Gurinskas sold the winery to Diamond Estates, which also owns Birchwood Estates and recently created a partnership with EastDell Estates and Thomas & Vaughan Estate Winery combining all four wineries under one company.

Winemaker Thomas Green, who studied under Gurinskas, is now building his reputation as one of Canada's bright stars in the wine business.

Selections include: Chardonnay, Riesling, Pinot Gris, Gamay Noir, Pinot Noir, Merlot, Cabernet blends.

Ridgepoint Wines
3900 Cherry Avenue, Vineland.
1-905-562-8853. www.ridgepointwines.com
Fri., Sun., Mon. 10 a.m. - 5 p.m., Sat. 10 a.m. - 6 p.m.

A recent addition to the wineries of Vineland, Ridgepoint opened its doors in 2003 just around the corner from Vineland Estates Winery. Set on the slopes of the Niagara Escarpment, this small farm gate winery is owned by Mauro and Anna Scarsellone. As one the first grape growers in Ontario to successfully plant Nebbiolo, a native Italian red wine grape, the Ridgepoint offers an eclectic variety of wines.

Selected Tastings: Chardonnay, Riesling, Merlot, Cabernet Sauvignon, Nebbiolo.

Royal DeMaria Wines
4551 Cherry Avenue, Vineland.
1-905-562-6767. www.royaldemaria.com
April – October Mon. - Fri. 11 a.m. - 6 p.m.,
Sat 10 a.m. - 6 p.m., Sun. 11 a.m. - 5 p.m.;
November – March By appointment.
Guided Wine Tour: *By appointment.*

Winemaker and owner Joseph DeMaria has a passion for Icewine. His winery is the only one in Canada dedicated to the sweet nectar of winter. He's bet the farm on crafting Canada's best known wine export. As an amateur winemaker, DeMaria has been producing Icewine since 1993. In 1998, he launched his first line of VQA Icewines and almost immediately established himself as one of the top producers of the sweet wine.

Self-proclaimed as Canada's Icewine Specialists, Royal DeMaria has won a number of international awards including VinItaly, VinExpo and Concours Mondial. In fact in 2002, Royal DeMaria become the first winery in the history of France's VinExpo, the world's most prestigious wine competition, to win five gold medals in one category.

In addition to the more popular Icewine styles of Vidal and Riesling, Royal DeMaria also features Icewines made of Merlot, Cabernet Franc, Cabernet Sauvignon and a Meritage, the world's first Bordeaux-styled Icewine blend of Cabernet Sauvignon, Cabernet Franc and Merlot. If you're looking to sample Icewine, Royal DeMaria should be on your list.

Selections include: Icewine.

Stoney Ridge Estate Winery
3201 King Street, Vineland.
1-905-562-1324. www.stoneyridge.com
June – October Daily 10 a.m. - 6 p.m.;
November – May Daily 10 a.m. - 5 p.m.
Guided Wine Tour: *July – September*
Daily 11:30 a.m. and 2:30 p.m.; October – June Weekends 11:30 a.m.

Stoney Ridge has a rich role in the history of Niagara's modern wine industry. Founded in 1985 by one of Canada's most accomplished winemakers, Jim Warren, the winery has moved around until finally finding its home in a house on the Beamsville Bench.

With a reputation built by Warren in its early days, Stoney Ridge is known for its vast array of small batch, high quality wines. A newly renovated retail facility offers cosy wine country charm. The wines are crafted by Liubomir Popovici whose style style has garnered many awards over the past few years. Warren recently rejoined the Stoney Ridge winemaking team, crafting the winery's Jim Warren Signature Series of premium wines.

Something unique to Stoney Ridge is a wine library that showcases the winery's history through a collection of a hundred different limited edition wines and back vintages. It traces the winery's history from the earliest days in 1985 spanning 18 years of its winemaking and wines that are available for purchase.

Selections include: Chardonnay, Riesling, Pinot Grigio, Cabernet Franc, Pinot Noir, Baco Noir, Cabernet Merlot.

Vineland Estates Winery
3620 Moyer Road, Rural Road 1, Vineland.
1-905-562-7088. www.vineland.com
Daily 10 a.m. - 6 p.m.
Guided Wine Tour: *May – November Daily 3 p.m.; December – April Weekends 3 p.m.*
Winery Restaurant: Restaurant at Vineland Estates Winery. *Open daily for lunch and dinner. Closed Mon. - Tues. January – April.*

Recognized as one of the pioneers of the wine industry along the Niagara Escarpment, Vineland Estates was established in 1988. German winemaker and nurseryman Hermann Weis had a vision of creating a Riesling that would stand up to those from the vineyards of his native Mosel, Germany. Based on the mineral-rich soils on the Escarpment, and the microclimate conditions of the vineyards, Vineland Estates quickly emerged as Niagara's premium Riesling producer.

Weis sold the vineyards in 1992, and the wines are now in the hands of Brian Schmidt, who has been recognized at international wine competitions such as VinItaly and the London Wine and Spirits Competition and has brought home gold medals for his Chardonnays and Icewines. The stable of wines has grown to include single-vineyard Chardonnays, Gewürztraminer, Pinot Gris, Pinot Blanc and a select roster of Bordeaux-style red wines.

With a reputation built by quality, Vineland Estates winery is also one of the most attractive sites in Niagara. The Moyer Road site's 1845 farmhouse accommodates the winery restaurant and the 1857 stone carriage houses the venue for winemaker dinners and private functions. An old barn was converted to mirror the architecture of the existing buildings and now is a tasting room and wine shop boutique.

The winery restaurant, which was one of the first winery restaurants in Canada, is one of the region's culinary highlights. It specializes in creating a dining experience that draws on the strengths of regionally sourced produce and meats and Vineland Estates wines. On a clear day, the view from the restaurant stretches past rolling vineyards, Lake Ontario and all the way to the cityscape of Toronto.

Selections include: Riesling, Chardonnay, Pinot Blanc, White Meritage, Pinot Noir, Cabernet Franc, Merlot, Cabernet Sauvignon, Meritage, Late Harvest Riesling, Riesling Icewine, Vidal Icewine.

Willow Heights Estate Winery
3751 King Street, Vineland.
1-905-562-4945. www.willowheightswinery.com
May – November Mon. - Sat. 10 a.m. - 5:30 p.m.;
Sun. and Holidays 11 a.m. - 5 p.m.;
December – April Mon. - Sat. 10 a.m. - 5 p.m.,
Sun. 11 a.m. - 5 p.m.
By appointment.

The Speranzini family founded Willow Heights Estate Winery in 1994. Similar to some other wineries in Niagara, Willow Heights is the creation of an amateur winemaker turned professional. Ron Speranzini established a reputation as a quality part-time vintner winning a number of awards for his wines. With some encouragement, Speranzini traded in his day job, and launched his first series of VQA wines in 1994. Since then, his wines have continued to receive rave reviews.

Housed in a Mediterranean-themed building, just a few kilometers from the village of Vineland, the winery features a patio offering an antipasto menu throughout the summer.

Selections include: Chardonnay, Riesling, Gamay Noir, Cabernet Sauvignon, Merlot, Tresette (Bordeaux-blend), Vidal Icewine.

Accommodations

Grimsby

Kittling Ridge Winery Inn & Suites
4 Windward Drive, Grimsby.
1-877-446-5746. www.krwineryinn.com
Located across the QEW from the Kittling Ridge Winery. Features

deluxe rooms, with conference and banquet facilities for up to 350 persons and a roof top lounge overlooking Lake Ontario.

Super 8 Motel
11 Windward Drive, Grimsby.
1-866-501-7666. www.super8grimsby.com
The recently opened Super 8 is situated right off the QEW in Grimsby. Close to the Niagara Escarpment wineries. Forty minutes from Niagara Falls and Niagara-on-the-Lake.

Jordan

Best Western Beacon Harbourside Inn & Conference Centre
2793 Beacon Boulevard, Jordan.
1-888-8-BEACON. www.bestwestern.com
Overlooking Lake Ontario, the Beacon Harbourside is best accessed from the Jordan Avenue exit off the QEW. Minutes from wineries in Jordan and Vineland and 20 minutes from Niagara Falls and Niagara-on-the-Lake. On-site restaurant with view of Lake Ontario. Boat docking available at marina.

Inn on the Twenty
3845 Main Street, Jordan.
1-800-701-8074. www.innonthetwenty.com
The Inn on the Twenty offers a luxurious stay. Each room is uniquely decorated and features luxury bedding, a fireplace, Jacuzzi tub and more. Spa services available. Located in the heart of Jordan Village across from Cave Spring Cellars and On the Twenty Restaurant.

Niagara Falls

Americana Conference Resort & Spa
8444 Lundy's Lane, Niagara Falls.
1-800-263-3508. www.americananiagara.com
Features include a 2,250-square-metre indoor waterpark with wave pool, eight water slides, kiddie pool, giant tipping bucket and

more, all under a retractable roof. Also includes a full service European spa.

Days Inn Clifton Hill/Casino
5657 Victoria Avenue, Niagara Falls.
1-800-461-1251. www.niagarahospitalityhotels.com
This new boutique-style hotel is in the heart of the Niagara attractions. Located steps away from the Casino Niagara, it's an easy walk to the Falls, Parkway and Clifton Hill.

Days Inn Fallsview
6408 Stanley Avenue, Niagara Falls.
1-800-263-2522. www.daysinn.ca
Virtually next door to the Skylon and Minolta Towers and minutes from the Falls, the location makes it a popular choice. Located directly across the street from the new Fallsview Casino Resort.

Doubletree Resort Lodge & Spa Fallsview
6039 Fallsview Boulevard, Niagara Falls.
1-800-222-TREE. www.niagarafallsdoubletree.com
This new resort offers well-appointed rooms and well-trained staff. Located a few blocks from the Fallsview Casino and the Falls, it also features the Five Lake Aveda Day Spa, an indoor/outdoor pool and a restaurant.

Embassy Suites Niagara Falls Fallsview
6700 Fallsview Boulevard, Niagara Falls.
1-800-420-6980. www.embassysuitesniagarafalls.com
The Fallsview Hotel stands 42 storeys above the brink of Niagara Falls. Located 90 metres from the edge of the water, rooms facing the Falls offer an unobstructed view. Walking distance to Niagara Fallsview Casino.

Hilton Niagara Falls
6361 Fallsview Boulevard, Niagara Falls.
1-888-370-0325. www.niagarafallshilton.com
Offers a spectacular view of the Falls and is located directly across the street from the Fallsview Casino. Many deluxe rooms and

suites have a full view of the Falls. Hotel also features a 900-square-metre indoor pool, encompassing whirlpools, a three-storey waterslide and waterfall.

Marriott Niagara Falls Fallsview & Spa
6740 Fallsview Boulevard, Niagara Falls.
1-888-501-8916. www.niagarafallsmarriott.com
Located on the brink of the Falls and across from the Niagara Fallsview Casino, the Marriott Fallsview & Spa has luxurious guestrooms, including whirlpool and fireplace, with a view of the Falls. Featuring a full service spa, dining room and even a chapel overlooking the Falls.

Niagara Fallsview Casino Resort
6380 Fallsview Boulevard, Niagara Falls.
1-888-FALLSVUE. www.fallsviewcasinoresort.com
Opened in 2004, the Niagara Fallsview Casino Resort features a hotel above the casino gaming centre. Modelled after Las Vegas-style casino resorts, Fallsview includes Galleria shopping centre, conference facilities, a variety of restaurants and a concert hall. The deluxe rooms include a panoramic view of the Falls.

Oakes Hotel Overlooking the Falls
6546 Fallsview Boulevard, Niagara Falls.
1-877-THE-OAKES. www.niagarahospitalityhotels.com
Holds the distinction of being the closest hotel to the Horseshoe Falls. The Oakes Hotel is also adjacent to the Niagara Fallsview Casino. Features an indoor pool, whirlpool, sauna, room service, bell service and superb dining in the hotel restaurant.

Old Stone Inn
5425 Robinson Street, Niagara Falls.
1-800-263-6208. www.oldstoneinn.on.ca
Charming, historical inn minutes from the Falls and Fallsview Casino Resort. The Old Stone Inn features cosy, well-appointed guestrooms, indoor/outdoor pools, hot tub, lounge and a century-old dining room.

Renaissance Fallsview Hotel
6455 Fallsview Boulevard, Niagara Falls.
1-800-363-3255. www.renaissancefallsview.com
Located near the base of the Falls, Renaissance offers luxurious accommodations with beautiful views of the Falls. Features include a fine dining restaurant and pub and indoor pool. Walking distance to the Fallsview Casino and the Falls.

Sheraton Fallsview Hotel & Conference Centre
6755 Fallsview Boulevard, Niagara Falls.
1-800-618-9059. www.fallsview.com
Situated 270 metres from the Falls, the Sheraton Fallsview features more than 400 rooms, many of which offer a panoramic view of the Falls and Niagara River. Fine dining restaurant overlooks the Falls. Other features include full service conference facilities and indoor pool. Close to the Fallsview Casino.

Niagara-on-the-Lake

Anchorage Motel
186 Ricardo Street, Niagara-on-the-Lake.
1-905-468-2141. www.theanchorage.ca
Located a few blocks away from the Festival Theatre. Reasonable rates through the year. On-site restaurant.

Charles Inn
209 Queen Street, Niagara-on-the-Lake.
1-866-556-8883. www.charlesinn.ca
Built in 1832, the small Charles Inn recently underwent a renovation to its 12 rooms. Stately yet comfortable, all the rooms have fireplaces and many offer adjoining balconies. Located steps from the Niagara-on-the-Lake Golf Course, which is the oldest course in North America. On-site formal Victorian restaurant and pub. Summer dining on the veranda.

Colonel Butler Inn, Best Western
278 Mary Street, Niagara-on-the-Lake.
1-866-556-8882. www.uppercanadahotels.com
Recently designated a Best Western, the Colonel Butler Inn features 26 guestrooms, some with fireplaces. Other features include whirlpool spa, exercise room and lounge. Within walking distance of Jackson-Triggs Niagara Estate Winery.

Harbour House Hotel
85 Melville Street, Niagara-on-the-Lake.
1-866-277-6677. www.harbourhousehotel.ca
One of Niagara-on-the-Lake's newest boutique hotels, Harbour House is a luxurious accommodation located along the Niagara River. With its contemporary design highlighting a nautical theme, it offers a comfortable stay. Walking distance to the downtown and all three theatres. Most rooms feature a view of the Niagara River.

King George III Inn
61 Melville Street, Niagara-on-the Lake.
1-888-438-4444. www.niagarakinggeorgeinn.com
This two-storey inn, located across from the Niagara-on-the-Lake marina, offers a wonderful view of the Niagara river. Walking distance to the centre of Old Town and the Shaw Festival theatres. Open seasonally, April to October.

Moffat Inn
60 Picton Street, Niagara-on-the-Lake.
1-905-468-4116. www.moffatinn.com
The whitewashed two-storey inn is located across from Simcoe Park, just down from the Festival Theatre, above Tetley's Stone Grill.

Oban Inn
160 Front Street, Niagara-on-the-Lake.
1-866-359-6226. www.obaninn.ca
Another historic landmark in the Old Town, the Oban Inn has been around for more than 170 years. Although it was destroyed by fire in 1992, a renovation restored it to its original grandeur. The 26

rooms highlight a charming décor with a British influence. Other features include a dining room and lounge. Steps away from the Niagara River and Lake Ontario and a few blocks from Main Street.

Olde Angel Inn
46 Market Street, Niagara-on-the-Lake.
1-905-468-3411. www.angel-inn.com
First opened in 1789, the Olde Angel Inn was destroyed during the War of 1812 but was rebuilt in 1816 and is now one of North America's longest operating inns. Be advised that all rooms are located above the Angel Inn Pub, which features live music late into the night on weekends. There are two cottages beside the inn that are also available to rent. A stone's throw from the main street and steps away from Court House Theatre and Royal George Theatre.

Pillar and Post Inn
48 John Street, Niagara-on-the-Lake.
1-888-669-5566. www.vintageinns.com
Originally a bustling cannery, the historic Pillar and Post was renovated into one of Canada's most recognized and luxurious inns. It has been awarded the CAA/AAA Four Diamond award for both accommodation and dining and has also been designated a Five Star Resort by Canada Select. Each guest room has a fireplace. Spa services are available. Walking distance to downtown and theatres.

Prince of Wales Hotel
6 Picton Street, Niagara-on-the-Lake
1-888-669-5566.
www.vintageinns.com
Considered the heart of the Old Town, the Prince of Wales Hotel has been in operation since 1864. Things have changed a little since its early days as a hitching post; the hotel is now considered one the finest in the country. This opulent hotel is decorated to reflect the

local British history and each room is beautifully furnished. Spa services and on-site restaurant and lounge.

Queen's Landing Inn
155 Byron Street, Niagara-on-the-Lake.
1-888-669-5566. www.vintageinns.com
Although a relatively new building in Niagara-on-the-Lake, Queen's Landing Inn was designed to blend in with the surrounding historical architecture. Located on the banks of the Niagara River, the stately hotel features marble flooring, a sweeping spiral staircase and stained glass ceilings. On-site restaurant and lounge. Close to Festival Theatre and walking distance to downtown.

Riverbend Inn and Vineyard
16104 Niagara Parkway, Niagara-On-The-Lake.
1-888-955-5553. www.riverbendinn.ca
Recently opened, Riverbend Inn is located in a country mansion along the Niagara Parkway. The original home was built in 1860 and has been restored to capture its former grandeur. Overlooks vineyards and the Niagara River the inn features 21 rooms and a restaurant. Just on the outskirts of the Old Town, it's a scenic walk to downtown and is situated beside Peller Estates Winery.

Royal Park Hotel
92 Picton Street, Niagara-on-the-Lake.
1-800-511-7070. www.uppercanadahotels.com
Located across from the Festival Theatre, Royal Park is a quaint hotel with suites featuring fireplaces and Jacuzzis. Dining offered in the modern restaurant, Zees Patio and Grill.

Victorian Suites Inn
1391 Niagara Stone Road, Niagara-on-the-Lake.
1-888-717-6600. www.victoriansuitesinn.com
Located just outside of the small town of Virgil, Victorian Suites is the closest inn to Hillebrand Estates. All six rooms have a décor to match the rich English history of the area and offer such luxuries as fireplaces and jet hydrotherapy tubs. A short car ride from downtown Niagara-on-the-Lake.

White Oaks Resort
253 Taylor Road, Niagara-on-the-Lake.
1-800-263-5766. www.whiteoaksresort.com
Off the QEW at the Glendale exit, White Oaks is a glamorous hotel. One of the highest ranking resorts in Ontario, the service is impeccable and the rooms are well appointed. Features include indoor pool, tennis facility, upscale restaurant and spa services. Ten minutes from downtown Niagara-on-the-Lake and Niagara Falls. Royal Niagara Golf Course and Niagara College's Teaching Winery are across the road.

St. Catharines

Comfort Inn St. Catharines
2 Dunlop Drive, St. Catharines.
1-800-4-CHOICE. www.choicehotels.ca
Exit the QEW at Lake Street and follow the North Service Road to the Comfort Inn. There are no bells and whistles but it is clean and affordably priced. The attached Golden Griddle restaurant is good for breakfast.

Days Inn
3305 North Service Road, St. Catharines.
1-800-544-8313. www.daysinn.niagara.com
Exit Victoria Avenue from the QEW, Days Inn offers an affordable stay. Close to wineries in Jordan, Vineland and Beamsville. Twenty minutes from Niagara Falls and Niagara-on-the-Lake.

Four Points by Sheraton
3530 Schmon Parkway, St. Catharines.
1-800-368-7764. www.fourpointsuites.com
Located on top of the Niagara Escarpment in St. Catharines, Four Points is best accessed by the HWY 406, which exits off the QEW. Features a restaurant and conference facilities. Twenty minutes to Niagara Falls and Niagara-on-the-Lake.

Holiday Inn
2 North Service Road, St. Catharines.
1-877-688-2324. www.stcatharines.holiday-inn.com
Recently renovated and right off the QEW at Lake Street in St. Catharines, the Holiday Inn is 10 minutes from Jordan Village, Niagara Falls and Niagara-on-the-Lake. Features include high-speed Internet, indoor/outdoor pools and restaurant.

Howard Johnson Hotel & Conference Centre
89 Meadowvale Drive, St Catharines.
1-877-688-2324. www.howardjohnsonstcath.com
Exit at Lake Street off the QEW. Affordably priced, featuring a sports bar and 24-hour restaurant. Ten minutes to Jordan Village, Niagara Falls and Niagara-on-the-Lake.

Quality Hotel Parkway Convention Centre
327 Ontario Street, St. Catharines.
1-877-688-2324. www.qhparkway.com
Completely renovated a few years ago, the Quality Hotel features a restaurant, lounge, billiards, video games, 40-lane bowling centre, high-speed Internet and fitness area. Minutes from downtown St. Catharines, Port Dalhousie and 10 minutes from wineries on the Niagara Escarpment, Niagara Falls and Niagara-on-the-Lake.

Dining

THE EMERGENCE OF NIAGARA AS A CULINARY DESTINATION follows the rise of the wine industry. A natural progression, many chefs in the area strive to pair the wines of Niagara with dishes that reflect the area's agricultural surroundings. From the first winery restaurant that opened more than 15 years ago, there are a number of fine dining establishments, and even causal offerings, located throughout the area. Included are establishments in Beamsville, Jordan, Niagara Falls and Niagara-on-the-Lake in wine country, the neighbouring city of St. Catharines and the small hamlet of Fonthill. Entrée price range: **Budget**: less than $15, **Moderate**: $16 to $24; **Upscale:** more than $25. The pricing information presented is based on the cost of a single dinner entrée, excluding taxes, tip and wine. Although the information provided has been verified, it's subject to change and it's best to contact the establishment prior to your visit.

Beamsville

The Restaurant at Peninsula Ridge
5600 King Street, Beamsville.
1-905-563-0900, ext 35. www.peninsularidge.com
Lunch Thurs. - Sat., dinner Wed. - Sun., Sun. brunch.
Reservations recommended; summer patio. **Upscale**

When executive Norm Beal decided to return to his roots in Niagara and open a winery, he didn't spare any expense. Often quoted as saying, "to make a million dollars in the winery business you need to spend $10 million," Beal did just that. He not only outfitted the winery with state-of-the-art gadgets, he refurbished an old farmhouse and converted it into an upscale restaurant combining fines wines with dishes made from locally grown produce. The two-level restaurant offers an intimate setting and great views of the vineyards. There is also a coach house that can be booked for private functions.

The View Restaurant at EastDell Estates Winery
4041 Locust Lane, Beamsville.
1-905-563-9463, ext 27. www.eastdell.com
Lunch, dinner Wed. - Sun., Sun. brunch.
Reservations required. **Moderate**

Tucked away on the Niagara Escarpment, The View serves as a casual dining spot with a picturesque view of both the rolling vineyards and Lake Ontario. Operated as part of EastDell Estates, it's a blend of rustic charm with local flavours. With hardwood floors, floor-to-ceiling windows and a central fireplace for those cold winter nights, it's a cosy restaurant.

Fonthill

Wild Flower Restaurant
219 Highway 20 East, Fonthill.
1-905-892-6167. www.wildflowerrestaurant.com
Lunch Wed. - Sat., dinner Wed. - Sun.,
Sun. brunch, afternoon tea 12 p.m. - 4 p.m. **Moderate**

    Located on old Highway 20, Wild Flower has been a fixture on the local culinary scene since 1996. Owned by Wolfgang Sterr, an internationally trained chef, the restaurant specializes in modern regional cuisine to complement the Niagara wines that dominate the wine list. Features regular winemaker's dinners and gourmet picnics during the summer.

Zest
1469 Pelham Street, Fonthill.
1-905-892-6474. www.zestfonthill.com
Lunch Tues. - Fri., dinner Tues. - Sat.
Reservations recommended. **Upscale**

    With an interior that reflects a modern, contemporary feel, Zest is an unexpected gem. Showcasing the wine country experience, Zest's menu highlights cuisine based on local seasonal ingredients and knowledgeable service. In-depth wine list features a wide selection from Niagara wineries.

Jordan

Beacon Harbourside Restaurant
2793 Beacon Boulevard, Jordan.
1-888-823-2266. www.bwbeacon.com
Breakfast, lunch, dinner daily. **Moderate**

    The restaurant, which faces the water, offers a great view of Lake Ontario. The menu is a combination of surf and turf and local, seasonally inspired dishes. Although the wine list is limited, it does feature a selection of Niagara wines. On a clear day the view extends across the lake to Toronto's CN Tower and Rogers Centre (formerly The SkyDome).

Butterball's Restaurant
2980 Regional Road 81, Jordan.
1-905-562-4328.
Breakfast, lunch, dinner daily. **Budget**

Situated at the base of the Twenty Valley basin, this rustic restaurant is located between Stoney Ridge Estate Winery and the village of Jordan. Butterball's is where the locals go for breakfast. On weekends a flea market sets up beside the restaurant.

On the Twenty Restaurant
3836 Main Street, Jordan.
1-905-562-7313. www.innonthetwenty.com
Lunch, dinner daily.
Reservations required. **Upscale**

The first winery restaurant in Niagara, On the Twenty, situated beside the Cave Spring Cellars tasting room, has earned its reputation as one of the best culinary experiences in Niagara. This beautifully styled restaurant offers fine dining with a menu that embraces local flavours and seasonal ingredients. The wine list features current and back vintages from Cave Spring, and some of the finest Niagara wines available. Dining area overlooks the stunning Twenty Valley basin.

Zooma, Zooma Café
3839 Main Street, Jordan.
1-905-562-6280.
May - December Lunch, dinner daily;
January - March Lunch, dinner Wed. - Sun. **Budget**

The funkiest café in the area, Zooma, Zooma's retro '50s style has a relaxed atmosphere. Located on the main street in Jordan Village, it features lunch dishes for those looking for something quick, yet delicious. Affordable and casual. Its limited wine list is all VQA.

Niagara Falls

Carpaccio Restaurant and Wine Bar
6840 Lundy's Lane, Niagara Falls.
1-905-371-2063. www.carpacciorestaurant.com
Lunch Mon. - Fri., dinner daily. **Moderate**

Carpaccio offers a casual dining experience with a focus on wine. The extensive wine list features a wide selection of Niagara wines as well as international offerings. The décor and menu reflect the comfortable atmosphere. Affordably priced.

Casa Mia
3518 Portage Road, Niagara Falls.
1-905-356-5410.
Lunch Mon. - Fri., dinner daily.
Reservations recommended. **Moderate/Upscale**

Located off the beaten path in Niagara Falls, contemporary and elegant Casa Mia has established itself as a culinary destination. The wine cellar is an attraction in itself featuring floor-to-ceiling racks that showcase more than 200 labels, many of them rare and collectible. Executive Chef Claudio Mollica has earned a reputation as one of Niagara's most creative chefs and his menu is close to his Italian roots. Impeccable service.

Casa d'Oro
5875 Victoria Avenue, Niagara Falls.
1-877-296-1178. www.thecasadoro.com
Lunch Sun. - Fri., dinner daily. **Moderate**

This family-operated restaurant has been a fixture for fine food and wine for more than 35 years. Wine list offers a large selection of Niagara and international wines. Located within walking distance to Niagara Falls.

Monticello Grille House and Wine Bar
5645 Victoria Avenue, Niagara Falls.
1-800-843-5251. www.monticello.ca
Lunch, dinner daily. **Moderate**

A perennial winner of the Wine Spectator Award of Excellence, Monticello specializes in Louisiana-style cuisine. Located in the heart of Niagara Falls and is walking distance of both casinos.

Pinnacle Restaurant
6732 Fallsview Boulevard, Niagara Falls.
1-905-356-1501. www.niagaratower.com
Breakfast, lunch, dinner daily. **Upscale**

Recently renovated restaurant perched on the top of the Konica Minolta Tower offers a stunning view of the Falls, complete with a wide view of the Niagara River. Fine selection of local wines and a menu to complement the scenery.

17 Noir
6380 Fallsview Boulevard, Niagara Fallsview
Casino Resort, Niagara Falls.
1-888-FALLSVUE. www.fallsviewcasinoresort.com
Dinner daily. Reservations recommended. **Upscale**

17 Noir is on the second floor of the Fallsview Resort Casino. Polished red, black and gold steps lead to the restaurant, which is decorated in roulette wheel colours. One of Niagara's top culinary attractions, 17 Noir has a spectacular view of the Falls, impeccable food and service, and the most extensive wine list in Niagara.

Skylon Tower
5200 Robinson Street, Niagara Falls.
1-888-839-7023. www.skylon.com
Lunch, dinner daily. **Upscale**

The dining room is located at the top of the tower overlooking the Falls. It features a revolving dining room offering a panoramic view of Niagara Falls and the surrounding area. The menu caters to a wide range of tastes and the wine list features a very limited selection of Niagara wines.

The Watermark Restaurant
6361 Fallsview Boulevard, Niagara Falls.
1-905-353-7138.
Breakfast, lunch, dinner daily. **Upscale**

Located on the Hilton Hotel's 33rd floor, The Watermark features floor-to-ceiling windows overlooking the Falls. This is one of Niagara Falls' top culinary attractions, with its contemporary design, modern fare and impressive local and international wine list.

Niagara-on-the-Lake

Buttery Theatre Restaurant
19 Queen Street, Niagara-on-the-Lake.
1-905-468-2564. www.thebutteryrestaurant.com
Lunch, dinner daily. **Upscale**

Located in the heart of the Old Town, the Buttery Theatre Restaurant offers a casual, comfortable dining experience. On weekends the restaurant hosts a King Henry VIII-themed dinner theatre production. Fine selection of Niagara wines.

Cannery Restaurant at the Pillar and Post Inn
48 John Street, Niagara-on-the-Lake.
1-888-669-5566. www.vintageinns.com
Breakfast, lunch, dinner daily.
Reservations recommended. **Moderate**

The Cannery Restaurant is a relaxed dining spot featuring country-style cooking and a seasonal menu. Large fireplaces make for a cosy setting during the winter months. This casual restaurant has a well-trained staff and completely Niagara wine list.

The Epicurean
84 Queen Street, Niagara-on-the-Lake.
1-905-468-3408. www.epicurean.ca
Lunch, dinner daily. **Moderate**

The Epicurean is a delightful bistro with a relaxed atmosphere that complements the made-to-order sandwiches and fresh salads. The long, narrow design also features a Provence-inspired dining room in the back. Ideal for a quick lunch or casual dinner before the theatre or after a day of wine touring.

Escabeche at Prince of Wales Hotel
6 Picton Street, Niagara-on-the-Lake.
1-888-669-5566. www.vintageinns.com
Lunch, dinner, afternoon tea daily.
Reservation recommended. **Upscale**

The jewel in the Vintage Inns crown, Escabeche is one of Niagara's most noteworthy dining establishments. Located inside the historic Prince of Wales Hotel, Escabeche features creative culinary dishes with an extensive vintage-dated Niagara wine list. Professional wait staff and sommeliers offer exceptional service. Regal décor with an English flare sets the mood in the dining area that looks out onto Queen Street. Minutes from all the theatres and shops in the Old Town. The Churchill Bar is ideal for drinks after a day on the Wine Route.

Hillebrand's Vineyard Cafe
1249 Niagara Stone Road, Niagara-on-the-Lake.
1-905-468-7123. www.hillebrand.com
Lunch, dinner daily.
Reservations recommended during summer. **Upscale**

One of the oldest winery restaurants in Niagara, Hillebrand's Vineyard Café is a culinary destination. Chef Tony DeLuca, one of Canada's leading chefs, has created a renowned dining experience that captures the essence of Niagara wine country. The wide selection of Hillebrand wines complements the food. View overlooks the vineyards.

LIV @ White Oaks
253 Taylor Road, Niagara-on-the-Lake.
1-905-688-2032, ext 5248. www.whiteoaksresort.com
Breakfast, lunch, dinner daily.
Reservations recommended. **Upscale**

Located on the outskirts of Niagara-on-the-Lake, LIV is part of the White Oaks Resort. The four-diamond restaurant showcases a modern design and features a globally influenced menu. A winner of the Cuvee Award for Best Ontario Wine List.

The New Italian Place Restaurant
186 Ricardo Street, Niagara-on-the-Lake.
1-905-468-2141.
Lunch, dinner daily. **Moderate**

Formerly known as the Anchorage Pub, this local favourite offers a casual dining experience with affordably priced Italian dishes. Located right across from the Niagara River, walking distance from Main Street in the Old Town and around the corner from the Queens Landing Inn.

Niagara Culinary Institute at Niagara College
135 Taylor Road, Niagara-on-the-Lake.
1-905-641-2252, ext 4619.
Lunch Tues. - Sun., dinner Wed. - Sat. **Moderate**

The Niagara Culinary Institute features a working restaurant for training students. A restaurant in the round, it offers a view of the college's vineyards and the Niagara Escarpment. Food is prepared by student chefs under the guidance of professors, and menu changes daily. Great prices for the quality of the dishes. Wine list offers a selection of Niagara wines including the College's own wines.

The Old Firehall Restaurant
268 Creek Road, Niagara-on-the-Lake.
1-905-262-5443.
Lunch, dinner daily. **Moderate**

At the four corners in the little hamlet of St. Davids, on the outskirts of Niagara-on-the-Lake near Queenston, you'll find The Old Firehall. Affordably priced, casual dining with a select Niagara wine list. Surrounded by a few antique shops and close to Château des Charmes.

The Olde Angel Inn Restaurant
224 Regent Street, Niagara-on-the-Lake.
1-905-468-3411. www.angel-inn.com
Lunch, dinner daily. **Budget/Moderate**

Casual dining in an Old English pub. The Olde Angel Inn is one of North America's oldest pubs. Includes formal dining and bar areas. Decent selection of Niagara wines. Located in the heart of the Old Town, minutes from the Royal George Theatre and the Court House Theatre.

Peller Estates Winery Restaurant
290 John Street, Niagara-on-the-Lake.
1-905-468-4678. www.peller.com
Lunch, dinner daily.
Reservations recommended; patio seating in summer. **Upscale**

High, vaulted ceilings and oversized windows face the winery's vineyards. Peller Estates Winery Restaurant captures the essence of dining in wine country with an elegant and stylish interior and regionally inspired menu. Wine list comprised mostly of Peller wines. Exceptional service. Walking distance to the Festival Theatre.

Ristorante Giardino
142 Queen Street, Niagara-on-the-Lake.
1-905-468-3263. www.gatehouse-niagara.com
Lunch, dinner daily.
Reservations recommended. **Upscale**

Located on the corner of Queen Street and Gate Street, Ristorante Giardino is inside the Gate House Hotel. Stylish decor influenced by Italian architecture reflects its authentic Italian menu. Wine list features both Niagara and international wines. Impeccable service.

Riverbend Inn and Vineyard
16104 Niagara Parkway, Niagara-on-The-Lake.
1-905-468-8866. www.riverbendinn.ca
Breakfast, lunch, dinner daily.
Reservations recommended; summer patio with vineyard view. **Upscale**

The stately Riverbend Inn offers an elegant dining experience amid the majestic Georgian-influenced architecture. The intimate dining room has 26 seats. Local seasonal cuisine and extensive Niagara wine list. Exceptional service. Situated on the Niagara Parkway, close to the Festival Theatre.

The Shaw Café and Wine Bar
92 Queen Street, Niagara-on-the-Lake.
1-905-468-4772. www.shawcafe.ca
Lunch daily, dinner daily. **Moderate**

A circular two-storey café with an outdoor patio overlooking the main street of the Old Town. With a casual dining atmosphere and a European café-style menu to match, it's a great place for a light lunch before crossing the street to the Royal George Theatre for a play. Features a wide selection of Niagara wines.

Shaw's Corner Lounge
The Oban Inn, 160 Front Street, Niagara-on-the-Lake.
1-905-468-2165. www.obaninn.ca
Breakfast, lunch, dinner daily.
Reservations recommended. **Moderate**

Just off Queen Street, in the heart of the Old Town, the Oban Inn offers a great view of the Niagara River spilling into Lake Ontario. A fire almost destroyed the historic inn, but it has since been beautifully restored. Design reflects the rich English tradition that defines the area. Local ingredients highlight traditional English cuisine with a modern twist. A lounge area is a great place to relax after touring or the theatre. Oban Inn also offers a more upscale dining experience in their Kir diningroom. Minutes away from all three festival theatres.

Stone Road Grille
238 Mary Street, Garrison Plaza, Niagara-on-the-Lake.
1-905-468-3474. www.stoneroadgrille.com
Lunch Tues. - Fri.; dinner Tues. - Sun. **Moderate**

    A local favourite. This funky restaurant features local produce and eclectic and stylish décor. Wine list is 100 per cent Niagara and there are plenty of wines offered by the glass.

Tetley's Steak & Stone
60 Picton Street, Niagara-on-the-Lake.
1-905-468-4641.
Lunch, dinner Wed. - Sun. **Moderate**

    A block away from the Shaw Festival, Tetley's is located underneath the Moffat Inn. Specializing in Swiss fondue dishes, it's a unique, casual dining experience. Wine list features mostly Niagara-on-the-Lake wineries.

Tiara Dining Room at Queen's Landing Inn
155 Byron Street, Niagara-on-the-Lake.
1-888-669-5566. www.vintageinns.com
Lunch, dinner daily.
Reservations recommended; patio in the summer. **Upscale**

    Located inside the regal Queen's Landing Inn, the elegant dining room has a view of the Niagara River. Chef Stephen Treadwell, a British-born, French-trained chef has done a masterful job in developing the reputation of the Tiara Dining Room as a gastronomical experience. Exceptional service. The Bacchus Lounge at the inn offers more casual dining. Minutes from Festival Theatre.

Terroir La Cachette
1339 Lakeshore Road, Niagara-on-the-Lake.
1-905-468-1222. www.lacachette.com
Lunch, dinner daily.
Reservations recommended. **Upscale**

    Although Terroir La Cachette is located inside the Strewn Winery, it is independently owned by chef Alain Levesque. The small, intimate setting captures the subtlety of Chef Levesque's French Provencal-style cuisine.

Zees Patio and Grill
92 Picton Street, Niagara-on-the-Lake.
1-905-468-5715. www.zees.ca
Lunch, dinner daily. Summer patio. **Moderate**

Zees Patio and Grill is located across from the Festival Theatre, the largest of the Shaw theatres. Casual dining with a wide selection of dishes and an extensive Niagara-on-the-Lake wine list.

St. Catharines

The Keg Steakhouse & Bar
344 Glendale Avenue, St. Catharines.
1-905-680-4585.
Dinner daily. **Moderate**

The Keg Steakhouse is located inside an old rubber factory just off HWY 406. In the 1850's, the building was known as the Beaver Cotton Mills (and later Merritton Cotton Mills). In 1881, the mill burned down and was replaced with an impressive red sandstone structure, which was the home to a number of companies, including the rubber factory. The beautifully restored building is a landmark in St. Catharines. This location offers a wide selection of Niagara wines.

La Scala Ristorante
26 Church Street, St. Catharines.
1-905-684-5448.
Lunch Mon. - Fri., dinner Mon. - Sat. **Upscale**

Located on Church Street, which got its name from the abundance of historical churches on the street. The popular Italian bistro is located in a small whitewash row house and features regional Italian dishes. The wine list features some Niagara wines with a wide selection of Italian offerings.

Mai Vi
55 St. Paul Street, St. Catharines.
1-905-988-1426.
Lunch Mon. - Sat., dinner daily. **Budget**

A modern Vietnamese restaurant located on the corner of St. Paul Street and William Street in downtown St. Catharines in the old Woolworths department store. Specializing in authentic Vietnamese cuisine, Mai Vi is one of St. Catharines' hot spots. Plenty of Niagara wines to chose from to complement the menu.

Olson Food & Bakery
17 Lock Street, St. Catharines.
1-905-938-8490.
Open daily.

Anna Olson, host of the popular show *Sugar* on Canada's Food Network and author of a dessert book by the same name, owns this bakery and gourmet food shop in Port Dalhousie. Daily dessert features and fresh bread have made Olson Food & Bakery a favourite destination for gourmands. Located inside the small boutique shopping centre, Lock and Main.

Pow Wow
165 St. Paul Street, St Catharines.
1-905-688-3106.
Lunch, dinner Mon. - Sat. **Moderate**

This is one of St. Catharines' most popular dining establishments. It features exposed brick, tin ceilings and two dining areas. The menu selection is a fusion of West Coast and Asian cuisine. Awarded best VQA Niagara Wine List by the Niagara Wine Festival, Pow Wow also features winemaker's dinners during the winter. Great service and a casual atmosphere. Participates in the bring-your-own-wine program, which allows the customer to bring in professionally made wine to be enjoyed with their dinner.

Sahla Thai Restaurant
288 St. Paul Street, St. Catharines.
1-905-704-0984.
Lunch Mon. - Fri., dinner daily. **Budget**

Serving authentic Thai cuisine. Popular with local foodies. Limited Niagara wines.

Touch of India
126 St. Paul Street, St Catharines.
1-905-988-1155.
Lunch Mon. - Sat., dinner daily. **Budget**

Authentic Indian cuisine in the heart of downtown St. Catharines. The emphasis here is on the cuisine, not the décor, and if you're looking for some Indian food during your trip through wine country, Touch of India won't disappoint.

Twelve - A Waterfront Grill
61 Lakeport Road, St. Catharines.
1-905-934-9797.
Summer Lunch Thurs. - Sun., dinner daily;
Winter Closed.
Reservations recommended. **Moderate**

Although annexed by St. Catharines a long time ago, residents in this hamlet still prefer to say they live in Port Dalhousie. Twelve is located in Port Dalhousie just beyond the bridge that links the sleepy historic town to the rest of St. Catharines. Casual with a nautical decorating theme, Twelve makes good use of the local produce. Offers an extensive Niagara wine list.

Vino Primo
67 St. Paul Street, St. Catharines.
1-905-688-4479.
Dinner Tues. - Sat. **Upscale**

Contemporary and stylish, Vino Primo offers an upscale dining experience that brings together Niagara's best wines and local flavours. The long, narrow restaurant features portraits of Niagara's winemakers hanging on the walls. Great service and knowledge staff.

Wellington Court Café
11 Wellington Street, St. Catharines.
1-905-682-5518.
Lunch, dinner Tues. - Sat. **Upscale**

A culinary institution in Niagara, Wellington Court has been around for more than 30 years. Owned since its inception by the Peakcock family, chef and owner Erik Peacock is one of Niagara's most accomplished chefs. The 40-seat restaurant offers an intimate setting and seasonal menu and has been featured in a number of national magazines including *Vines*. Highlights include winemaker's dinners and a seasonal, locally inspired menu. Participates in the bring-your-own-wine program.

Vineland

Lake House Restaurant and Lounge
3100 North Service Road, Vineland.
1-905-562-6777. www.lakehouserestaurant.com
Lunch Mon. - Sat., dinner daily, Sun. brunch. **Moderate**

Located inside an old farmhouse that was built in 1867 by the Moyer family, the building offers one of the best views of Lake Ontario. Features include three fireplaces and original woodwork. Causal dining featuring a large selection of menu options and an extensive VQA wine list. Summer patio facing the lake is an ideal spot to watch the sun set.

Laurie's Orchard Café
4100 Victoria Avenue, Vineland.
1- 905-562-7771.
Breakfast and lunch Tues. - Sun., dinner Thurs. - Sun. **Budget**

Located on Victoria Avenue, which links the QEW to the main street in Vineland, Laurie's Orchard Café is situated in a small plaza. It's a simple place to stop for a quick bite and the servings are generous. Wine list features affordably priced Niagara wines.

Old Oak Country Market
4600 Victoria Avenue, Vineland.
1-905-562-3039.

Old Oak Country Market specializes in upscale fresh produce. Housed in a replicated gabled barn with red wood finish and white roof, it features an impressive selection of local nuts, seasonal local fruit, fresh bread, artisinal cheeses and meats. A great place to stop for snacks or to create gourmet picnics to enjoy at one of the many scenic parks in the area.

Vineland Estates Winery Restaurant
3620 Moyer Road, Vineland.
1-888-846-3526, ext 33. www.vineland.com
Lunch, dinner daily.
Reservations recommended; patio in the summer. **Upscale**

The restaurant at Vineland Estates has been a wine and culinary destination for more than a decade. With arguably the most scenic view of the countryside, it captures the essence of Niagara's wine country. Located inside a renovated country home with exposed posts and beams, polished pinewood floors and large windows, the restaurant is a blend of rustic charm, exceptional service and seasonal menus.

Also Notable:

Edgewater Manor
518 Fruitland Road, Stoney Creek.
1-905-643-9332.
Lunch, dinner Mon. - Sat. **Upscale**

Edgewater Manor is located in a restored turn-of-the-century home on the shore of Lake Ontario. Edgewater offers formal service, a good selection of VQA wines and features local seasonal menu. Spectacular view of the lake.

Shopping

TO COMPLEMENT A TOUR OF WINE COUNTRY, THERE'S A host of boutique stores and shopping centres across Niagara. Whether you're taking a break between tours, looking for a unique gift, or simply want to indulge yourself with something special, you'll be able to find it in Niagara. Hours of operation exclude holidays. Although the information provided has been verified, it's subject to change, please call ahead.

NIAGARA-ON-THE-LAKE

Beamsville

Niagara Presents
4516 Mountainview Road, Beamsville.
1-905-563-1777. www.niagarapresents.net
Mon. - Sat.
Specializing in food products made from locally grown produce, Niagara Presents offers a wide range of foods including jams and jellies for sampling and purchase, as well as gift baskets. Open to the public, tours are available of the facility, which is located near Mountain Road Wine Company.

Jordan

Main Street Jordan
Hours of individual stores may vary.
Although small in size, the village of Jordan offers an eclectic range of shops to complement the fine wines of Cave Spring Cellars. Stores include women's clothing, home and garden, antiques and art.

Niagara Falls

Canada One Factory Outlet
7500 Lundy's Lane, Niagara Falls.
1-866-284-5781. www.canadaoneoutlets.com
Open daily.
Located just a few minutes from the base of Niagara Falls, Canada One features such outlet stores as Sony, Nike, The Body Shop Depot, Club Monaco, Danier Leather, Ecco Shoes, Guess, Liz Claiborne, Jones New York, Reebok, Samsonite, Tommy Hilfiger, Villeroy & Boch and many more.

Fallsview Galleria
6380 Fallsview Boulevard, Fallsview Casino Resort,
Niagara Falls. www.discoverniagara.com
Open daily.

Located inside the Fallsview Casino Resort, the upscale stores of Galleria include Danier Leather, Linda Lundström, Swarovski, Bentley, Philippe Artois and more.

Newville Classic Candles
4605 Kent Avenue, Niagara Falls.
1-905-356-4112, ext. 360. www.newville-candles.com
Open daily.
Newville Classic Candles offers a selection of handmade and custom candles for purchase.

Souvenir City
4199 River Road, Niagara Falls. 1-866-344-0985.
Open daily.
This is the ultimate place to grab a remembrance of your trip to Niagara Falls. Located along the scenic Niagara Parkway, it's the largest souvenir store in the region.

Niagara-on-the-Lake

Shops of the Old Town
Niagara-on-the-Lake
Hours of individual stores vary.
The Niagara-on-the-Lake Heritage District, often referred to as Old Town, features buildings dating back 200 years. Stroll down the street for storefront shopping that captures a past era. Boutique shops include Maple Leaf Fudge, The Scottish Shop, Angie Strauss Fashions, and many more.

Kurtz Orchards Market
16006 Niagara Parkway, Niagara-on-the-Lake.
1-905-468-2937. www.kurtzorchards.com
Open daily.
Located on the Niagara Parkway just outside of the Old Town, Kurtz Orchards captures the essence of Niagara's agricultural roots. This Niagara icon features local produce and other local specialty foods such as jams and preserves.

Picard Peanuts
801 East / West Line, Niagara-on-the-Lake.
1-905-468-2455. www.picardpeanuts.com
Open daily 10 a.m. – 5 p.m.
Specializing in gourmet nuts, especially locally grown varieties. Situated beside Joseph's Estate Winery.

St. Catharines

Downtown St. Catharines
Hours of individual stores vary.
The boutique shops of St. Paul Street and James Street, in the historic mercantile district of St. Catharines, offer an experience that captures the spirit of downtown storefront shopping. Specialty stores include Elliot and Co., White on White, Gifted Presence, Not Just Art, Jordin Stewart, BB Blooms and many more.

Pen Centre
Highway 406 at Glendale Avenue, St. Catharines.
1-800-582-8202. www.thepencentre.com
Open daily.

The largest indoor shopping centre in Niagara features 180 stores including popular names like The Gap, Roots, HMV, Sears, Old Navy and many more.

The Shops of Lock and Main
St. Catharines
A collection of specialty shops, including Olson's Food & Bakery, dot the intersection of Lock Street and Main Street in Port Dalhousie between the Lions Tavern and Kilt and Clover Pub.

Border Shopping

DUTY FREE SHOPS

Niagara Duty Free Shop
5726 Falls Avenue, Niagara Falls.
1-877-642-4337. www.niagaradutyfree.com

Peace Bridge Duty Free
Peace Bridge Plaza, Fort Erie.
1-905-871-5400. www.dutyfree.ca

Peninsula Duty Free
Queenston Lewiston, Niagara Falls.
1-905-262-5363. www.dutytaxfree.com
Open 365 days of the year.
Located at each border crossing on the Canadian side, Duty Free Stores offer tax-free retail shopping for a wide variety of products including Niagara wines. Also featured at the outlets are GST Rebate centres for U.S. travellers who can claim GST back from purchases made in Canada. All major credit cards accepted.

Nature Trails and Sites

THROUGHOUT NIAGARA, A SERIES OF NATURE TRAIL RUN both along the Niagara Escarpment and along the Niagara River. Taking the time to appreciate the natural beauty of the area will complement the wine country experience.

Bruce Trail
www.brucetrail.org
The Bruce Trail is Canada's oldest and longest continuous footpath. It runs along the Niagara Escarpment from Niagara to Tobermorey covering more than 850 km of trail and provides the only public access to the magnificent Niagara Escarpment. It has been designated a protected UNESCO World Biosphere Reserve, one of only 12 such reserves in all of Canada.

Dufferin Islands
www.niagaraparks.com
Trails invite leisurely walks through 11 small islands, to wonderful areas where it is possible to view dozens of bird species. The Dufferin Islands are an excellent location to enjoy a peaceful picnic lunch. Anglers of all ages enjoy the fishing (catch and release program). During the annual Winter Festival of Lights, from mid-November to mid-January, Dufferin Islands comes to life with numerous colourful, light displays.

Floral Clock
14004 Niagara Parkway, Queenston.
www.niagaraparks.com
A popular stop on the Niagara Parkway, the Floral Clock is a working clock. One of the largest in the world, it measures 12.2 metres in diameter, and features more than 20,000 small plants, all placed closely together creating elaborate designs. Designs are changed twice a year.

Journey Behind the Falls
6650 Niagara Parkway, Niagara Falls.
www.niagaraparks.com
This year-round attraction affords thrilling views from below and behind the thundering Falls. Visitors descend 46 metres by elevator, where a short tunnel gives access to two outdoor observation decks and two portals located directly behind the Falls.

NATURE TRAILS AND SITES

Maid of the Mist Steamboat
5920 River Road, Niagara Falls.
1-905-358-5781. www.maidofthemist.com
May – November.
The *Maid of the Mist* takes you to the brink of the Falls for a spectacular view and a full appreciation for the sheer power of the water crashing over the precipice. Be prepared to get a little wet from the mist, but rain gear is provided for the trip.

Niagara Circle Route
www.regional.niagara.on.ca
The Niagara Circle Route connects Lake Ontario and Lake Erie as it follows the Welland Canal and Niagara River, forming a circular route. The paved path is almost complete, and it is great for walking, hiking, running, in-line skating and cycling.

Niagara Escarpment
www.niagaraescarpment.org
The Escarpment is one of Canada's most scenic landforms. It winds 725 km from Queenston, near Niagara Falls, to the islands of Fathom Five National Marine Park in Tobermory, Ontario. The Escarpment originated more than 450 million years ago as part of the ice age. A protected area, the Escarpment is a World Biosphere Reserve as designated by the United Nations. The presence of the Escarpment plays an important role in the cycle of grape growing in Niagara.

Niagara Falls
Niagara Parkway, Niagara Falls.
www.niagaraparks.com

Once a military post, now a year-round travel destination, the Canadian Falls attracts daredevils and honeymooners alike. The Canadian Falls is 53 metres high and the river is an astounding 56 metres deep. Many attractions and tours make for better viewing of the falls and its whirlpool rapids including the *Maid of the Mist* Steamboat, Journey Behind the Falls and Whirlpool Aerocar.

Niagara Falls Aviary
5651 River Road, Niagara Falls.
1-866-994-0090. www.niagarafallsaviary.com
An oasis of feathers with more than 300 tropical birds featured in this facility. Birds fly freely throughout the aviary. Featuring interactive and educational programs. Located just down the road from the brink of the Falls.

Niagara Glen Nature Area
Niagara Parkway, Niagara Falls.
www.niagaraparks.com
Located just north of the Falls, opposite Whirlpool Golf Course. The Niagara Glen is a unique area on the Niagara River, carved out between 7,000 and 8,000 years ago. The Niagara Glen presents a fascinating study in rare flora, Carolinian forestry and is also a very important birding area. Hikes through the Niagara Glen involve an elevation change of more than 60 metres. Proper footwear, suitable for steep and rugged terrain is required. Guided Rim Tours also provide an informative, easy stroll along the top of the Glen.

Niagara Parks Botanical Gardens
2565 Niagara Parkway, Niagara Falls.
www.niagaraparks.com
Located along the Niagara Parkway, north of the Falls, the Botanical Gardens are designed and maintained by students at the School of Horticulture, Canada's only residential school for horticulturists. In between wine tours, explore 40 hectares of horticultural heaven, including a stunning rose garden with more than 2,300 plant varieties, an arboretum, herb garden and more.

Niagara Parks Butterfly Conservatory
2405 Niagara Parkway, Niagara Falls.
www.niagaraparks.com *Open year-round.*
Located close to the Niagara Parks Botanical Garden on the Niagara Parkway, the Butterfly Conservatory features more than 2,000 tropical butterflies that fly free in a glass-enclosed rain forest setting complete with waterfalls and pools.

Niagara Parks Recreation Trail
www.niagaraparks.com

This trail system follows the path of the Niagara River from Fort Erie to Niagara-on-the-Lake, a full 58 km through beautiful parkland, over small bridges and sprinkled with strategic lookouts. Take time to read some of the more than 100 historic plaques along the trail that honour the memory of significant persons, places and events that make up the rich history of Niagara.

Oakes Garden Theatre
Niagara Falls.
1-905-357-9340. www.niagaraparks.com
Located on the north side of Clifton Hill between Falls Avenue and River Road. This Greco-Roman–style amphitheatre is nestled in a setting of rock gardens, lily ponds, terraces and promenades, overlooking the American Falls. Owned and maintained by Niagara Parks, this is the site of numerous concerts and special events in the summer.

Queen Victoria Park
Niagara Parkway, Niagara Falls.
www.niagaraparks.com
A jewel in the crown of the Niagara Parks, Queen Victoria Park is located across from the American Falls at the brink of the

Horseshoe Falls. The well-landscaped Park offers fine views of the Falls and beautiful floral displays. The Park is illuminated at night, and is the centre for the annual Winter Festival of Lights, running from mid-November to mid-January. Queen Victoria Park is the main staging area for many events and the perfect spot to watch Friday and Sunday night fireworks throughout the summer.

Queenston Heights
14184 Niagara Parkway, Queenston.
www.niagaraparks.com
Queenston Heights Park is the site of a famous War of 1812 battle, during which Sir Isaac Brock was killed. A 50-metre monument erected in his honour is surrounded by greenspace that contains a large picnic area with open-air tables and covered pavilions, a band shell, tennis courts and hiking trails. Queenston Heights Park is located on top of the Niagara Escarpment and offers spectacular views of the lower Niagara River, surrounding countryside, Lake Ontario, and on a clear day the Toronto skyline. It was here that the Falls were first formed more than 10,000 years ago. The Bruce Trail also starts here.

Whirlpool Aero Car
3850 Niagara Parkway, Niagara Falls.
www.niagaraparks.com
Ride safely between two Canadian points in an open-air gondola high above the raging turbulent waters of the Niagara River Whirlpool. Operation depends upon wind and weather conditions.

Tours

TOURING NIAGARA WINE COUNTRY IS AS SIMPLE AS FOLLOWING the Wine Route signs from winery to winery, but for those looking for a more structured, and sometimes more adventurous experience, touring companies in Niagara offer a unique way to sip and savour the wines of the region. Most touring companies require advance booking and planning.

Crush on Niagara Wine Tours
Beamsville.
1-866-408-WINE. www.crushtours.com
Crush on Niagara specializes in small, customized tours. Based in Beamsville, the company offers small and medium size tours in large vans throughout the Niagara region. The company also owns a small bed and breakfast, which is located on the Wine Route in Beamsville.

Niagara Airbus
8626 Lundy's Lane, Niagara Falls.
1-800-268-8111. www.niagaraairbus.com
A full transportation company, Niagara Airbus offers more than just airport services. With a fleet of customized vans and buses, the company has a selection of wine tours across Niagara. Offers packaged tours of wineries in Niagara-on-the-Lake and Niagara Escarpment.

Niagara Getaways
37 Barnsdale Lane, St. Catharines.
1-800-667-9538. www.niagaragetaways.com
Customized wine tours to wineries in Niagara-on-the-Lake. Corporate and social programs offered throughout the year. Programming also includes multi-day wine tour packages including overnight accommodations and visits to other attractions.

Niagara Helicopters
3731 Victoria Avenue, Niagara Falls.
1-800-281-8034. www.niagarahelicopters.com
Offering an exciting view of wine country, Niagara Helicopters offers winery-focused tours including landing in vineyards for a grounded winery tour. Small groups only.

Niagara Nature Tours
Rural Road 1, Vineland Station.
1-888-889-8296. www.niagaranaturetours.ca
Specializing in eco-friendly tours, Niagara Nature Tours focuses on hikes through vineyards and wineries on the Niagara Escarpment.

Niagara Wine Tours International
92 Picton Street, Niagara-on-the-Lake.
1-800-680-7006. www.niagaraworldwinetours.com
Located in Niagara-on-the-Lake, Niagara Wine Tours offers cycling and van tour packages covering the entire region. In operation since 1992, the company offers professional services to accommodate large and small groups. Although a cycling tour of wineries may sound like a daunting task, a number of wineries are clustered together, making the trips between manageable.

Steve Bauer Bike Tours
4979 King Street, Beamsville.
1-905-563-8687. www.stevebauer.com

After a successful cycling career, Niagara's own Steve Bauer operates a bike tour company featuring guided bike excursions of Niagara's wine country. The customized day-long tours are available for social and corporate groups. Advance booking is required. Tour packages cover both Niagara-on-the-Lake and the Niagara Escarpment.

Wine Country Tours
2755 Hurricane Road, Rural Road 2, Welland.
1-905-892-9770. www.winecountrytours.ca
Specializing in custom tours throughout Niagara wine country suited for corporate and social groups.

Zoom Leisure Bicycle Tours and Rentals
42 Market Street, Niagara-on-the-Lake.
1-866-811-6993. www.zoomleisure.com
Located beside the Olde Angel Inn in the Old Town, Zoom offers packaged cycling tours of Niagara-on-the-Lake, which include custom wine tours. Zoom also offers bike rentals for those looking to go at their own pace.

Historical Sites

NIAGARA IS A RICH PART OF CANADA'S HISTORICAL FABRIC. Niagara-on-the-Lake was the first capital of Ontario. The region was a major battleground in the War of 1812 between the Americans and the British. The Welland Canal, an engineering marvel, which connects Lake Ontario and Lake Erie, was first opened in the mid-1880s. The city of St. Catharines was a major fur trading centre and mercantile district.

Brock's Monument
14184 Niagara Parkway, Queenston Heights Park, Queenston. www.niagaraparks.com
Open year-round.
Historically significant, this was the site of one of the key battles of the War of 1812. Before dawn on October 13, 1812, an American army crossed the Niagara River to attack the British forces stationed in the village of Queenston. The town was of importance to the British, as it was where all supplies destined for the Upper Lakes were portaged around Niagara Falls. Despite General Isaac Brock's death early in the battle, his troops won. His leadership during the war is recognized at this monument, which is perched on the cliffs of the Niagara River facing the United States.

Butler's Barracks / The Common
King Street and John Street, Niagara-on-the-Lake.
Open year-round.
Following the War of 1812, work began on new barracks and storehouses on the southwestern edge of the military lands, or Commons, out of reach of the American guns. Situated across the road from Fort George, by 1854 the site became known as Butler's Barracks, in honour of John Butler and his Rangers, Loyalist soldiers who had founded the town of Niagara towards the end of the American Revolution.

Chippawa Battlefield Park
Just off the Niagara Parkway, Niagara Falls.
www.niagaraparks.com
Open year-round.
For history buffs, the battlegrounds of the War of 1812 have been maintained in some areas of Niagara. The battlefield of Chippawa was the site of one of the largest engagements. In 1814, American, British, Canadian and Native soldiers clashed in one of the longest battles of the war. Each year in the vast, open field, a re-enactment takes place to mark the battle. Although off the Wine Route path, it's an interesting piece of Canadian history.

Fort George
Niagara Parkway at John Street, Niagara-on-the-Lake.
1-905-468-6614. www.pc.gc.ca
April - October.
One of the most important Forts built by the British to protect Upper Canada from an American invasion, Fort George was the headquarters for the Centre Division of the British Army during the War of 1812. The Fort, which has been fully restored and maintained, offers a first-hand look at life in the early 1800s complete with costumed staff. Overlooks the Niagara River. Within walking distance from the Old Town and Peller Estate Winery.

Fort Mississauga
Niagara-on-the-Lake. www.pc.gc.ca
April - October.
Located in the grounds of the Niagara-on-the-Lake Golf Course, Fort Mississauga is an example of a star-shaped earthwork fort, which means the earth has been mounded up to form a wall of defense against invading troops. The fort assisted in keeping the Americans from penetrating into Niagara during the War of 1812.

Laura Secord Homestead
29 Queenston Street, Queenston.
1-877-642-7275. www.niagaraparks.com
May - September.
A person of Canadian historical significance, Laura Secord provided valuable information to the British Army about an American invasion during the War of 1812, and in doing so helped keep Niagara under British rule. Her home, which has been restored, is located in the village of Queenston. Period-costumed guides provide details of Secord's trek as she travelled 32 km on foot to get the message to the British.

Lundy's Lane Historical Museum
5810 Ferry Street, Niagara Falls.
1-905-358-5082. www.lundyslanemuseum.com *Open daily.*

In the heart of Old Drummondville, the museum boasts a world-class collection of artifacts from the War of 1812. Also includes many other artifacts related to the founding and development of the city of Niagara Falls, Canada.

Mackenzie Heritage Printery & Newspaper Museum
1 Queenston Street, Niagara-on-the-Lake.
1-877-642-7275. www.mackenzieprintery.ca
May – October.
Located at the base of Queenston Heights, Mackenzie Heritage Printery is in the former home of political reformer William Lyon Mackenzie, who also published one of Upper Canada's first newspapers, *Colonial Advocate*. The small museum also features a working Linotype and eight operating heritage presses for visitors to explore.

McFarland House
15927 Niagara Parkway, Niagara-on-the-Lake.
1-877-642-7275. www.niagaraparks.com
May - October.

Located at McFarland Point Park along the cliffs of the Niagara River across from Lailey Vineyards, McFarland House captures the spirit of 1800s living. The Georgian-influenced home has been restored and visitors can enjoy the tea garden in the summer with a glass of Niagara wine. An idyllic spot for picnics.

Morningstar Mill & Mountain Mills Museum
2710 Decew Road, St. Catharines.
1-905-937-7210. www.morningstarmill.ca
May - October.
A restored 19th-century working grist mill and miller's house perched next to the picturesque Decew Falls on the Niagara Escarpment, just south of Brock University. Located just off the wine route, the closest winery is Henry of Pelham.

Niagara Apothecary
5 Queen Street, Niagara-on-the-Lake.
1-905-468-7932. www.niagarafoundation.com
May - September.
A National Historic Site located on Queen Street in the Old Town. The Niagara Apothecary has been recreated to illustrate how pharmacists applied their trade 100 years ago.

Sir Adam Beck 2 Generating Station
14000 Niagara Parkway, Niagara-on-the-Lake.
1-905-357-2379. www.opg.com
Open year-round.
The Sir Adam Beck is one of Ontario's largest hydroelectric plants that divert water from the Niagara River to power the station. A massive undertaking, it was built in 1958 and it remains an engineering marvel to this day. Tours offered.

Welland Canals Centre / St. Catharines Museum
1932 Welland Canals Parkway, St. Catharines.
1-800-305-5134. www.stcatharineslock3museum.ca
Open year-round.
Located at Lock 3 along the Welland Canal, the centre offers a viewing station of the lock to see the system that allows ships to navigate between Lake Ontario and Lake Erie. Also on-site is the St. Catharines Museum, which exhibits the history of St. Catharines throughout the year.

Arts

Grimsby

Grimsby Public Art Gallery
18 Carnegie Lane, Grimsby. 1-905-945-3246.
Mon. – Fri. 10 a.m. – 5 p.m., Tues. – Thurs. 10 a.m. – 8 p.m., Sat. – Sun. 1 p.m. – 5 p.m.
The Grimsby Public Art Gallery is located within the newly built library and art gallery complex located on Carnegie Lane. The Gallery was established in 1975, and is one of Niagara's leading galleries supporting the work of local artists.

Jordan

Jordan Art Gallery
3836 Main Street, Jordan.
1-905-562-6680.
Summer Mon. – Sun. 10 a.m. – 6 p.m.;
Winter Wed. – Sun. 10 a.m. – 5 p.m.
Features the works of Niagara-based artists.

Jordan Historical Museum of the Twenty
3800 Main Street, Jordan.
1-905-562-5242. www.jordanvillage.com
May – August Tues.- Sun. 10 a.m. - 5 p.m.;
Private functions year-round.
The Jordan Historical Museum features artifacts from the surrounding Twenty Valley area and is located in two beautifully restored historic buildings — an 1815 log farmhouse and an 1859 schoolhouse.

Ninavik Native Arts
3845 Main Street, Jordan.
1-800-646-2848. www.jordanvillage.com
Daily 10 a.m. – 6 p.m.
A 30 year-old gallery featuring art and crafts by Canadian Native artists.

Niagara Falls

Ochre Art Gallery
Doubletree Resort, 6039 Fallsview Boulevard, Niagara Falls.
1-800-730-8609. www.niagarafallsdoubletree.com
Opens Winter 2006; call for hours
Located inside the Doubletree Resort in Niagara Falls, the recently opened gallery features original paintings by Canadian artists that reflect the natural beauty of the Canadian outdoors.

Niagara-on-the-Lake / Queenston

Angie Strauss Art Gallery
129 Queen Street, Niagara-on-the-Lake.
1-888-510-0939. www.angiestrauss.com
Mon. – Tues. 10 a.m. – 5 p.m., Wed. – Thurs. 10 a.m. – 5:30 p.m., Fri. – Sat. 10 a.m. – 6 p.m., Sun. 10 a.m. – 5:30 p.m.
The gallery features watercolour and oil paintings, prints and cards by renowned Canadian artist Angie Strauss. Located in the heart of the Old Town.

The Artists' Loft
188 Victoria Street, Niagara-on-the-Lake.
1-905-688-4063. www.patriciapaquin.com
Daily 10 a.m. – 8 p.m.
Featuring the whimsical and functional ceramics of Patricia Paquin plus a wide selection of oil and watercolour paintings and prints by many of Niagara's outstanding artists.

Doug Forsythe Gallery
92 Picton Street, Niagara-on-the-Lake.
1-905-468-3659. www.dougforsythegallery.com
April – June Daily 10 a.m. – 5:30 p.m.;
July - September Daily 10 a.m. – 6 p.m.;
October – December 10 a.m. – 5 p.m.;
January – March Fri. – Sun. 10 a.m. – 5 p.m.
Etchings, engravings, woodcuts, cancelled intaglio plates, original watercolours, oils, mixed media and prints by Canadian artists Doug Forsythe and Marsha Forsythe. Located between the Moffat Inn and Royal Park Hotel, just down from the main street of the Old Town.

The King Street Gallery
153 King Street, Niagara-on-the-Lake.
1-905-468-8923. www.poulinart.com
Call for hours.
Featuring the works of renowned Canadian artist Chantal Poulin.

Pumphouse Visual Arts Centre
247 Ricardo Street, Niagara-on-the-Lake. 1-905-468-5455.
Summer Daily 1 – 4 p.m.;
Winter Fri. – Sun. 1 – 4 p.m.
Located in a restored 1891 water pumping station, the centre provides residents and visitors with an environment that encourages interest in a variety of visual art forms. Offers classes, workshops, lectures and exhibitions in a wide range of media are ongoing.

Riverbrink - Samuel E. Weir Gallery
116 Queenston Street, Queenston.
1-905-262-4510. www.riverbrink.org.
Summer Wed. – Sun. 10 a.m. – 5 p.m.
Situated on the Niagara River at the village of Queenston, the gallery overlooks the battlegrounds of The War of 1812. The Samuel E. Weir Gallery specializes in works pertaining to the history of the Niagara Region, portraits of the area's founders, as well as Canadian paintings including the Group of Seven, old Quebec silver, Indian artifacts, French Impressionist works and other unique pieces.

Romance Collection Gallery
177 King Street, Niagara-on-the-Lake.
1-800-667-8525. www.romancecollection.com
Tues. – Sat. 10 a.m. – 5 p.m., Sun. 1 p.m. – 5 p.m.
A fine collection of original art, limited edition reproductions and collectibles in a completely restored Victorian treasure. Features the works of Trisha Romance.

St. Catharines

Rodman Hall
109 St. Paul Crescent, St. Catharines.
1-905-684-2925. www.brocku.ca/rodmanhall
Mon. – Thurs. Noon – 9 p.m., Fri. – Sun. Noon – 5 p.m.
One of the premier facilities for the visual arts in the Niagara Region, Rodman Hall presents dynamic and diverse year-round exhibitions. Rodman Hall is a unique historic property along the Twelve Mile Creek in the centre of St. Catharines. Also the location of the Walker Botanical Gardens.

Performing Arts

Niagara Falls

Avalon Ballroom
6380 Fallsview Boulevard, Niagara Fallsview Casino Resort, Niagara Falls. 1-888-836-8118. www.discoverniagara.com
Located in the Niagara Fallsview Casino Resort, the Avalon Ballroom features top performers in an intimate setting.

Greg Frewin Theatre
**5781 Ellen Avenue, Niagara Falls.
1-866-779-8778. www.gregfrewintheatre.com**
Opened in 2005, this dinner theatre features Greg Frewin, one of Canada's top magicians. He has performed around in the world, including Las Vegas. The dinner show, which features wild animals and amazing feats of magic, is one of Niagara Falls' most popular entertainment attractions.

Oh Canada Eh? Dinner Show
**8585 Lundy's Lane, Niagara Falls.
1-800-467-2071.
www.ohcanadaeh.com**
Features comical plays depicting classic Canadian characters in a log cabin setting.

Niagara-on-the-Lake

Jackson-Triggs Niagara Estate Amphitheatre Series
2145 Regional Road 55, Niagara-on-the-Lake.
1-866-589-4637. www.jacksontriggswinery.com
Jackson-Triggs hosts an annual outdoor entertainment series, which features a range of pop music, symphony concerts and theatrical performances with dates in June, July and August.

Shaw Festival
10 Queen's Parade, Niagara-on-the-Lake.
1-800-511-7429. www.shawfest.com
One of the world's finest theatre companies, the Shaw Festival is an annual eight-month celebration, from April to November, of plays by Bernard Shaw and his contemporaries. Unique in terms of its focus, geographical reach and artistic development, The Shaw plays run in three theatres in Niagara-on-the-Lake.

Vineland

Twenty Valley Playhouse
3994 Victoria Avenue, Vineland.
1-866-440-0895. www.twentyvalleyplayhouse.com
Opened in the summer of 2005, the Twenty Valley Playhouse offers popular dinner theatre in a restored church on Victoria Avenue.

Glossary

WHEN TOURING THROUGH A WINERY, OR SIMPLY SAMPLING wine at the tasting bar, staff may use wine terms that are unfamiliar to many people. Below is a collection of wine related words and phrases that will make it easier to understand the world of wine.

Acid/Acidic
A tart, sour or fresh character, which has an impact on the body, balance and longevity of wine. Generally more obvious in, and more descriptive of, young white wines — where it gives balance and a crisp, clean taste.

Alcohol
Alcohol is what separates wine from grape juice. It is expressed as per cent by volume of the total liquid, and is a key flavour component and preservative. Canadian table wines generally range from 10 to 14 per cent.

Aroma
The range of scents found in a wine, including primary fruit aromas from the grape, secondary aromas from the winemaking process and tertiary aromas from bottle aging.

Balance/Balanced
A positive assessment of a wine's character, it refers to when all of the components are in harmony.

Barnyard/Farmyard/Stables
A descriptor for a decidedly complex and funky aroma found in some red wines. Despite the smell, these kinds of wines taste of heaven.

Barrel/Barriques
Wooden barrels, commonly produced by makers in France, the U.S., and to a lesser degree, Hungary and Yugoslavia, are made from oak staves and are toasted on the inside to help the aging of wine. With a lifespan of four or five years, barrels are expensive ($650 to $1,000 per 225 litre barrel) and are generally used only for wines with the inherent qualities for long-term cellaring. This is the major reason that "Barrel Aged," "Barrel Fermented" and "Barrel Reserve" wines cost you more. The newer the barrel, the more oak flavour imparted to the wine.

Barrel Aged
Wine that was aged, anywhere from a few months to several years, in a barrel after the completion of fermentation. Barrel aged wines have more noticeable oak characteristics than barrel fermented wines.

Barrel Fermented
Wine, usually whites (Chardonnay, Sauvignon Blanc or, in one rare case, Riesling) that are fermented in oak barrels rather than stainless steel or other kinds of fermentation tanks. It may come as a surprise that, although this process adds to the body and mouth-feel, it doesn't necessarily impart oak characteristics to the finished wine.

Blend
A wine that is blended from different grapes, vineyards, regions or vintages. It is a case of the whole being better than the sum of its parts, or when different wines are mixed together to create the best wine possible. The practice is most apparent in varietal wines such as Cabernet Merlot or Riesling Gewürztraminer, however almost every wine is a blend of some sort.

Body
The feeling of a wine on the palate, ranging from light to heavy (or full-bodied).

Botrytis Affected (BA)/Botrytis Cinerea
A beneficial rot that shrivels grapes and concentrates their flavour, sugar and acidity. Botrytis plays a role in some late-harvest wines and Icewines produced in Ontario and British Columbia.

Brix
Term for natural grape sugar, often an indicator of ripeness of the fruit. Warmer growing seasons produce higher sugar levels.

Brut
Refers to very dry wines, especially sparkling wine.

Buttery
Rich and creamy aroma, flavour and texture. It is often associated with malo-lactic fermentation, a winemaking process that converts hard, malic acid (green apple flavours) in wine to soft, lactic acid (rich, buttery flavours).

Cedar
Aroma found in wines that have been aged in oak barrels.

Character
Distinct attributes of a wine or grape variety.

Closed
Not revealing aromas or flavours. Aging and/or decanting can help a closed wine open up.

Creamy
A cream-like mouth-feel; doesn't imply a lactic flavour.

Cuvé Close
An affordable and quick fermentation technique for sparkling wine, in which the secondary fermentation takes place in a

reinforced stainless steel tank. Also known as the Charmat process.

Cuvée
A blend of wines from the same region.

Decanting
Pouring wine from the bottle into another container to aerate the wine and remove sediment, reserved almost exclusively for red wines other than Gamay and Pinot Noir.

Dry
No sugar or residual sweetness remaining (note that a fruity wine can be dry).

Dusty
Refers to the drying effect of tannins in red wine.

Earthy
Complex, appealing aromas and flavours like mushroom, flint, stone, dust and soil.

Estate Bottled
Labelling prerogative for wineries that grow, vinify and bottle grapes from their own vineyards, generally a sign of quality wine.

Finish
The final flavour impression a wine makes, ranging from short to long duration.

Firm
Describes the texture and structure of a wine, usually referring to young tannic reds that show great potential for the future.

Gamy
Meaty, slightly decaying aromas resembling game meats found in complex reds — another strangely appealing quality, given the right dosage.

Grassy
Aromas and flavours of fresh-cut grass or fresh herbs, most frequently used to describe Sauvignon Blanc.

Green
Tart flavours and textures, usually caused by unripened grapes.

Grip/Gripping
The firmness of tannin (red wine) or acidity (white) on the palate, considered a good indication of a well-made wine.

Herbaceous
A vegetal, grassy, herbal tone in aromas and flavours.

Icewine
Protected term for late-harvest wines that are produced from grapes that are naturally frozen on the vine.

Jammy
A rich, concentrated, semi-sweet fruit characteristic.

Late-Harvest
The source of much confusion on wine labels, this term has many uses. Essentially it means grapes were left on the vine after normal harvest time. Most late-harvest wines enjoy a dramatically increased sweetness and flavour, but not all.

Lean
A wine with more acidity than fruit.

Length/Lingering/Long
Measurement of a wine's final impression after swallowing. Many believe that the longer the finish, the better the wine.

Meritage
Rhymes with "heritage." An American term that describes red or white blended wines made in the fashion of Bordeaux. Generally a premium wine produced in small batches in better vintages.

Malo-lactic Fermentation
A secondary fermentation, used to soften some Chardonnay and red wines, in which the malic acid of the wine is converted to lactic acid.

Mouth-feel
Describes the texture of the wine on the palate.

Non-vintage
A wine produced by blending wines from different years, such as sparkling wines designed in a house style that is unchanging from bottle to bottle, year to year.

Nose
Describes the smells and aromas of a wine.

Old Vines
Wine produced from vineyards planted more than 15 years ago. The older a vine gets, the less fruit it produces. When there is less fruit on a vine the flavours, sugars and acidity are more concentrated.

Palate
Overarching term referring to both a wine's flavour and the tasting of wine in the mouth.

Petrol/Kerosene
Pungent, yet pleasant, gasoline and oil aromas most typical of maturing or mature Riesling.

Racy
Describes a lively, zesty acidity, most often found in Riesling and Sauvignon Blanc.

Reserve
Unregulated term that suggests the wine has received a lot of tender loving care from the winemaker. Ideally, it should be used to highlight a winery's best bottles.

Round
Smooth flavours and textures in a well-balanced wine.

Single Vineyard
Usually an indicator of premium quality, it means that 100 per cent of the grapes in a wine came from the same vineyard.

Smoky
Describes aromas of smoke generally imparted to the wine via oak aging.

Sur Lie or Sur Lee
French term for a winemaking technique of aging wine on the lees (spent yeast cells) to contribute a nutty, yeasty character.

Süssreserve
Refers to the winemaker reintroducing some unfermented grape juice into the wine before bottling. This adds some sweetness and can enhance the roundness of the mouth-feel.

Tannin
A dry, astringent texture derived from grapes and barrels that adds structure to full-bodied red wine.

Tart
Puckering acidity, considered a fault if excessive.

Terroir
A French term suggesting that certain vineyards impart a unique character to their wines, which cannot be duplicated anywhere else because the soil, wind, rain and other climatic conditions add their signatures to the finished wine. New World critics dismiss it as a marketing ploy, but a growing number of winemakers are subscribing to the theory.

Texture
Overall mouth-feel of the wine, including tannin, acidity, fruit extract and concentration.

Toasty
Pleasant aroma imparted from oak barrels.

Varietal
A wine named after its principal grape, such as Chardonnay or Cabernet Franc. According to the VQA it must contain at least 80 per cent of that grape and be blended with the other 20 per cent being made of accepted varieties.

Vintage
The year in which a wine's grapes were harvested. In the case of Icewine production, which often carries over into the next year, the vintage date does not roll over.

VQA
Vintners Quality Alliance. Winemaking standards, produced and legislated in Ontario and adopted in British Columbia, that cover designated growing regions, grape varieties and accepted practices.

Warm
Describes a wine with noticeable heat from its alcohol content. It is considered a fault if the perception surpasses warm and becomes hot.

Yeasty
Fresh doughy aromas and flavours, more acceptable when found in sparkling wine.

Zesty/Zippy
A lively and fresh acidity.

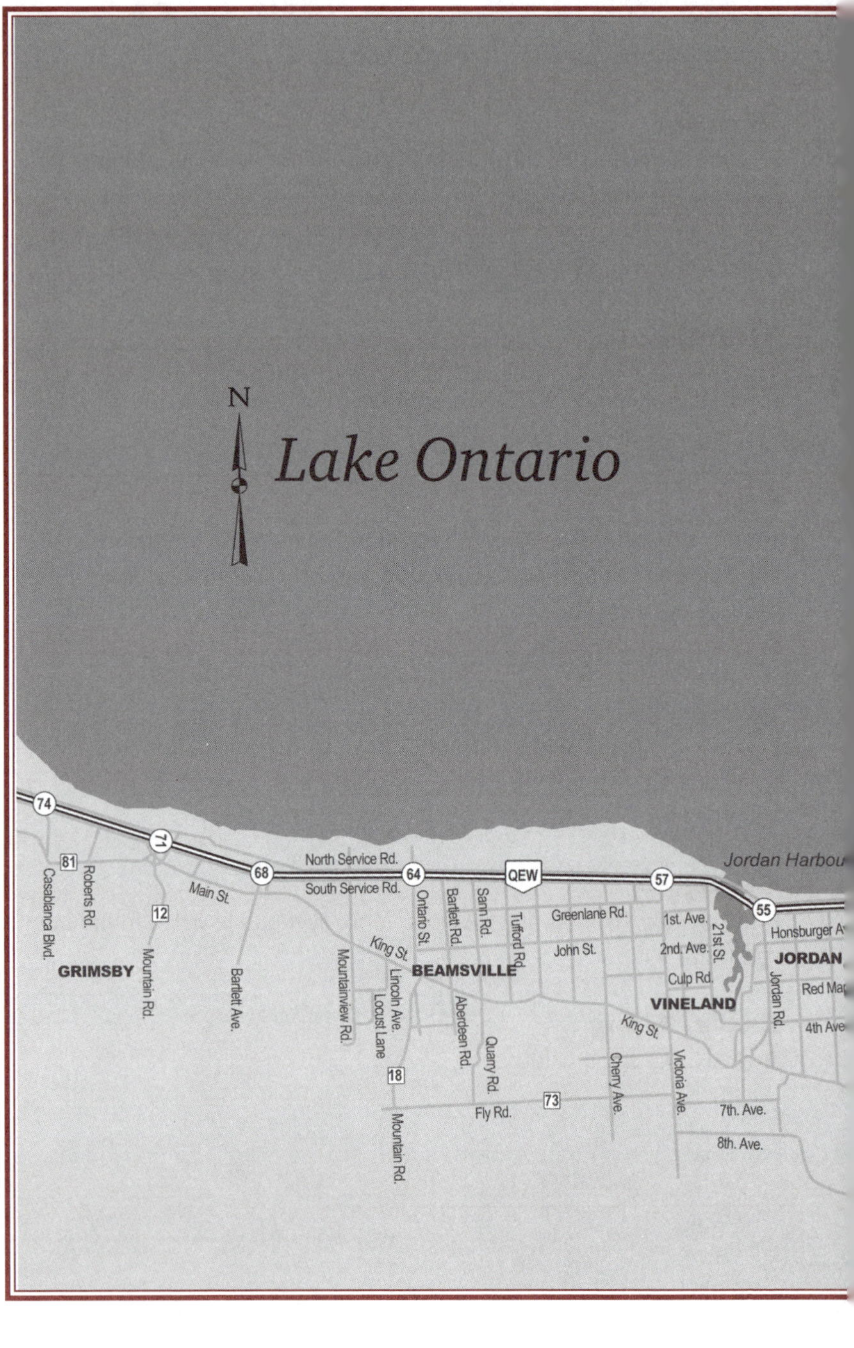
N
Lake Ontario
Jordan Harbou
74
71
81
68
64
QEW
57
55
North Service Rd.
South Service Rd.
Main St.
12
Casablanca Blvd.
Roberts Rd.
GRIMSBY
Mountain Rd.
Bartlett Ave.
Mountainview Rd.
King St.
Ontario St.
Bartlett Rd.
Sann Rd.
Tufford Rd.
Greenlane Rd.
John St.
1st. Ave.
2nd. Ave.
21st St.
Honsburger A
JORDAN
BEAMSVILLE
Lincoln Ave.
Locust Lane
Aberdeen Rd.
Culp Rd.
VINELAND
Jordan Rd.
Red Ma
4th Ave
King St.
Quarry Rd.
Cherry Ave.
Victoria Ave.
18
73
Fly Rd.
7th. Ave.
8th. Ave.
Mountain Rd.

Niagara Wine Region

MAP OF NIAGARA WINE REGION **123**

Copyright © 2005 by CanWest Books Inc., representing CanWest MediaWorks Publications Inc.

All rights reserved. No part of this book may be reproduced, stored in a retrieval system or transmitted, in any form or by any means, without prior written consent of the publisher or a licence from the Canadian Copyright Licensing Agency (Access Copyright). For a copyright licence, visit: www.accesscopyright.ca or call toll free to 1-800-893-5777.

Published by CanWest Books Inc.
A subsidiary of CanWest MediaWorks Publications Inc.
1450 Don Mills Road
Toronto, ON
Canada, M3B 2X7

Library and Archives Canada Cataloguing in Publication

Sendzik, Walter
  Insider guide to the Niagara wine region / written and fact checked by Walter Sendzik.

ISBN 0-9736719-6-3

  1. Wineries--Ontario--Niagara Peninsula--Guidebooks.
  2. Wine and wine making--Ontario--Niagara Peninsula.
  3. Niagara Peninsula (Ont.)--Guidebooks. I. Title.

TP559.C3S44 2006   663'.2'00971338   C2006-900010-7

Design & Composition: *Mad Dog Design Connection Inc.*
Cover Concept: *Mary Hughson*
Map Design: *Richard Pape*

Every attempt has been made by the author to contact copyright holders and ensure that all information presented is correct. In the event of omission or error, please contact the publisher.

Printed and bound in Canada by Tri-Graphic

First Edition

10 9 8 7 6 5 4 3 2 1

Photos included in this book courtesy of:

Niagara Economic and Tourism Corporation
Niagara Falls Tourism
Niagara Parks Commission
Wine Council of Ontario
City of St. Catharines
Niagara-on-the-Lake Chamber of Commerce
Shaw Festival

All photos are reprinted with permission for editorial purposes

NOTES

NOTES

NOTES